More Moxie than Money

THREE WOMEN - ONE COMPANY

Bernice Davidson

www.trafford.com

North America & international
toll-free: 1 888 232 4444 (USA & Canada)
fax: 812 355 4082

For all of our clients
past, present and future

Thank you for supporting us
and appreciating us

You are all in our mind's eye forever

TABLE OF CONTENTS

Foreword & Acknowledgements

FOREWORD

*T*his book is a labour of love. I loved my work and it brought me much satisfaction. I have found that the same is true of my predecessor and my successor and with a 50th anniversary looming on the horizon I wanted to put it on paper. For 50 years we have been making other people look good on paper and now it's our turn.

We all know about the huge failure rate for small business. How could a business survive for 50 years, moving location five times and with three different owners? Was the value in the concept? Well, the concept changed three times; it began as a secretarial service, and then became a packaged office, and finally an association management company. Also it has had two different names. How could it possibly be thriving with all these changes?

Perhaps there was something different about the three owners. Are we a rare breed? I think not but it bears examination and that is the search that brought this book to fruition. I hope to inspire others to find their satisfaction by living on the edge. In a small business nothing is ever taken for granted and you often must reach beyond your comfort level. Yet what satisfaction comes from finding that we really are capable of much more than our guidance teachers ever predicted for us.

Come along and see what steel is made of.

Bernice Davidson
North Vancouver
July 2007

MORE MOXIE than MONEY
THREE WOMEN - ONE COMPANY

ACKNOWLEDGEMENTS

I wish to thank Denize Callaway for creating Tri-C Secretarial Services Inc. and selling the company to me. I also wish to thank Donna Denham for purchasing the company and running it with such success. I am much indebted to both of them for their support and encouragement on this project. I am also indebted to our corporate sponsor, "Tri-C Secretarial Services Inc." doing business as "Support Services Unlimited", for sponsoring the publication of this book.

Chapter One
THE PLAYERS

This is the story of three women and the one company which has been owned by each of them in turn over a 50 year period. The women are not related and it was their work which brought them together.

What was it about such a company that appealed to each of these women? Why did they find it exciting to run their own show, rather than working for someone else? What did they have in common and what unique strengths did each bring to the business? Here's one little secret – none of them had a bankroll to begin with and they were all self-supporting.

The company began as Tri-C Secretarial Services (later became Support Services Unlimited) and for now we will refer to it as Tri-C. The woman who laid the foundation was Denize Callaway.

Denize – the Founder

PHOTO: LANCASTER GUARDIAN

1

Denize Callaway moved to Vancouver from Edmonton in 1951 and worked at Lever Brothers as secretary to the division manager for a year until she was offered a job at Kemano. A huge project was under way there to build a tunnel and power plant inside a mountain to serve Alcan, the aluminum company which was being constructed at Kitimat. In those years the Cold War between the U.S. and Russia looked as if it could become World War III at any time and Canada seemed like a logical battleground.

When she returned to Vancouver after 18 months, she worked as a secretary for McCormack's Biscuits for just over two years. Then on New Years Eve of 1956 her boss called her in and said "Denize, we're letting you go…and we're giving you two weeks pay." Of course she was devastated over the next few days; there weren't a lot of jobs and things were pretty tough in the late fifties. Denize talked to her friend Mickey McGuire and said, "I'm out of a job and what am I going to do?" Always her booster, he said, "You'll get a job".

It really wasn't so easy and she began working for a temporary agency. They placed her as secretary to the CEO of a company but there wasn't enough work to keep her busy. Even though they were paying the agency big money to have her there she was not fully utilized. One day she was paying invoices and could see that the temp agency was billing $10 an hour for her work, while they were paying her just $1.75 an hour. Suddenly she thought; "I'm on the wrong end of the stick. I think I'll go out and start my own business". That's when Denize decided to start a secretarial service. The question was – how to finance it?

Time now for some background: Denize was born in the Peace River country, the fourth of five children and the family moved to Edmonton when she was 10. Basketball became a passion during her teen years and her team became the Alberta provincial champions. Her mother taught her the value of volunteering and she became secretary of a club for the blind which set up the first Credit Union for the blind. Once they were able to secure credit it meant success and independence for their members.

When Denize finished secondary school she wanted to go to university but it was during World War II and her family didn't have the money. This left her with the option to attend a 10-month business college and then go to work. When she began the business in 1957 she had been working for 14 years at jobs that were both interesting and demanding. First Denize had worked for a steel plant and learned about manufacturing and procuring supplies. Next she was Girl Friday in a printing plant which did all the

DENIZE IN 1953 NEAR THE MOUNTAIN SUMMIT BETWEEN KEMANO AND KITIMAT

correspondence courses for students in BC and Alberta. From there she became secretary to the Edmonton Recreation Commission, and the work involved going to conferences and workshops. Then she went to work for the engineering department of the City of Edmonton for several years.

Denize's job experience had given her a good overall picture of industry. She could talk to people about setting up offices; she could talk to them about salesmen and salesmen's hours and setting up schedules, and ordering products. Now, at age 30, she had a fairly wide knowledge. She always found working easy – it was not a problem for her. Believe it or not, at one time she had been quite shy and found it hard to talk to people, but the business world had changed that.

Now in 1957 Denize was ready to go out and earn what she was worth, working for herself, rather than the $1.75 someone else would pay her.

Bernice – Changing Direction

Photo courtesy Ed Chan

Bernice Davidson came to Vancouver from Revelstoke, B.C. in 1978, where she had most recently run a fish and chip restaurant, then worked as a desk clerk at a hotel. She had married young, mothered four children, and then when the youngest was three, went to work full time.

She began as secretary to the personnel manager at McCulloch of Canada in Toronto, Ontario. After a move to Sarnia, she became the second staff trainer with Zellers in Canada. When the family moved to Vancouver she was able to continue her work with Zellers but the pay was minimal. Another search for a position in personnel found her at Weiser Lock in Burnaby, which lasted for a year. A move to Maple Ridge and she worked as a secretary at one of the secondary schools in the district, later worked at setting up the Resource Centre for School District 42, a new concept at the time.

A move to Quesnel and she worked at Canada Manpower, then to Prince George where she worked for the Town Planner, then on to Revelstoke and fish and chips. When her husband wanted to move to the Yukon she decided she'd had enough of his restless moving and left for Vancouver with her youngest daughter (now 16) to look for something more stable.

Bernice always said that the constant moving had prepared her children for future shock, and little did she realize that it was a great background for running a secretarial service. She is the eldest of four children, with the drive that usually goes with that position in the family. Her father was a dairy farmer near Toronto and her ex-husband had been in business twice, so she had some entrepreneurial background. Along the way she had determined that she wanted to earn a better than average living and now at age 42 was looking for a way to do so.

When Denize Callaway asked her if she would be interested in becoming a partner in Tri-C she was surprised, however as time went on she could see that the packaged office business was thriving and interesting. There was just one problem; she had no money beyond an RRSP of $1,000, not nearly enough to buy into the business in 1980.

Donna – Bringing Electronic Expertise

Donna Denham was almost 40 when she took over Support Services Unlimited from Bernice in June of 1998. She found it interesting that she was almost as old as the business, which had turned 40 in March of 1997.

Donna grew up in Vancouver, the younger of her parent's two daughters, and had begun working with computers when she was 18. Early training brought her good wages, flexibility in working hours and experience with almost every computer system in the city. Her most useful training came in a year-long pilot project at Capilano College called "info-tech", which was limited to 20 students. It was an evening course, ahead of its time, which taught web development, and a multitude of advanced PC/Mac based technologies.

Donna soon found that programming was not for her, however as she worked with a group of introverted programmers her social skills began to develop. She began as a "shy" person but learned to become the sales person who found out what the client needed, and then interpreted those needs to the programmers. When a program was completed she went back to the company and trained staff to use the new program. She soon had valuable communication skills under her belt.

Next was contract work for the government to improve the capability of databases in the early 1990's. She realized that the same programs used by government and large companies could be made affordable for smaller businesses and non profits. Donna helped a Notary Public computerize their transactions, and then remained in the notary's office, from there offering secretarial services to the general public. Soon three of her clients were non profit associations and she began to dream of setting up a business that provided small non profits with the latest in computer based programs.

One day she saw an "association management" business for sale. Knowing that this was her dream she had to see it and was soon face to face with Bernice Davidson.

After looking over the business she knew that she had to have it, but how? A single mother with three teen-age daughters, she did well to manage supporting her family and there was little left for savings.

A few days later she had lunch with "Hope".

Chapter Two
DENIZE THE FOUNDER

The Beginning

*O*nce I decided to begin a secretarial service I spoke with two friends who were both working, Marie Coffey and Georgina Cantalini, and asked them if they wanted to help form a company. When they agreed we chose the name "Tri-C Secretarial Services" to stand for we three women whose surnames began with "C". This was much easier to remember than our first choice: "Try Callaway, Cantalini & Coffey Secretarial Services". As both Marie and Georgina worked full time it was up to me to get the company organized. I think I was one of the first to ask people to bring work to my office, rather than sending employees out to work. It seemed to me to be a much more efficient way to handle it. The trend was to send people out to work in other offices and I reversed that trend.

I could never have done it on my own. I had neither money nor credit at the bank, because at that time I was living on $50 a week and paying about $13 for a bed-sitting room with a hot plate in it. It wasn't possible to save any money. I had a bit of money when we came out of Kemano but that didn't last too long because there weren't many jobs when we returned to Vancouver and it took a while to find work in those days.

The man in my life, Mickey McGuire, had a friend named Lloyd Muir, with a small office at the corner of Georgia and Cardero. It was across the street from the present Bayshore Inn, which opened four years later in 1961. I met with Lloyd, who was just starting out in public relations, a new field in those days. He had a lot of influential clients, among them the B.C.

Turf & Country Club. He said that if I wanted to come and work in his office and do the little bit of work he needed done, I could have the use of all the equipment in the office to do outside work for other people. So, I moved in with my only capital $50 in the bank.

The office was a little tiny place with a good address, the 1500 block of West Georgia Street. It held a regular manual typewriter and another with a long carriage, as well as a mimeograph machine and a two-line telephone. Mickey had great sales experience and I couldn't have had a better teacher to tell me how to go out and sell my new company. I just went to work and made calls and cried a little at night when I went home because I wasn't getting any business for the first few days.

One of the first clients was R.G. Morrow & Co., an accounting company on Broadway. I was typing financial statements that were huge and they required five copies. In those days there were no photocopy machines and no liquid paper to correct mistakes. It was necessary to use five sheets of paper and insert carbon paper between the pages; this resulted in one original and four copies. I'd begin to type and when there was a mistake I had to erase all five copies. This was not easy work. I was always on a deadline because these statements came in at the last minute. It was March when I started and everyone was trying to get their income tax in by the end of April. That was the start of it and for many years Tri-C faced that April tax deadline.

The hardest part was going in and knocking on doors and saying over and over again, "My name is Denize Callaway and I've just started a small secretarial service on the corner of Cardero and Georgia. You have a nice office here and I thought there might be times when you are overloaded with work or holiday times when you need someone to do something – could I talk to your manager?"

In some cases there was resistance and I would try to talk my way around that by saying, "Having worked myself I know that sometimes there is work to be done and you just can't stay and do it or you don't want to stay and do it. Well I'm right down the block and we're going to be working nights so you can just phone me and I can come and pick up your work and take it back to my office. You can go home and be with your family or do whatever you're doing that week-end and it will be all done when you come back to work."

Most of them thought that if it wasn't going to interfere with their job, they would have an option if they didn't want to work overtime so they would make an appointment for me to see the boss. The hardest part was getting by that barrier. Some nights I was exhausted because I wasn't a sales person, and I was so tired of telling my story and I would think, "This is never going to work. I'm never going to make any money. I'm going to starve to death." But I survived and I'm so happy I did. I guess my technique improved because before long there was the first job and the second job and before I knew it I was really busy.

Who Were The Clients?

There were a lot of young architects and engineers in 1957 just graduating from university after being in the services during the war, then returning to school to get their degrees. Many of them had gone to war with nothing more than an elementary education and when they returned it was to a different world where they were offered higher education. Once they had benefited from that education they had no desire to work for someone else and take orders as they had done in the service. They were now mature men, often with young families and many wanted to start their own businesses.

PAT CANNING, BILL RHONE AND MARLIES MCGUIRE, 1995

It was a great time for people wanting to do their own thing as Vancouver was beginning to boom and there was a lot of building going on. The young architects in the west end who were sharing offices with other people became pretty important clients. Some of them are still around today. One of those architects was Bill Rhone and he had just graduated from university when

Accounts Receivable

	Account	Job #	Now Quarter	Tax alle	Tax	Gross Inv	
	St. Mary's School	571	1200			1200	
	" "	571B	560			560	
	R. G. Morrow	572	455			455	
	" "	573	2705			2705	
	St. Mary's School	574	2400			2400	
	R. G. Morrow	575	645			645	
	R. G. Morrow	576	610			610	
	R. G. Morrow	5710	155			155	
	R. G. Morrow	5711	230			230	
	R. G. Morrow	5712	255			255	
	R. G. Morrow	5713	1870			1870	
	R. G. Morrow	5716	310			310	
	R. G. Morrow	5717	715			715	
	R. G. Morrow	5715	1875			1875	
			13925			13925	
	J. H. Mow					7600	
						23425	

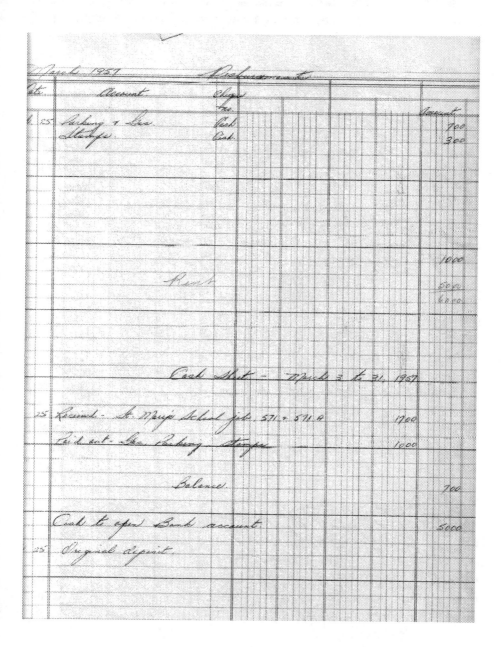

he came to Tri-C. He was a young man on his own and we did a lot of work for him and his firm, Rhone Iredale. When I retired in 1984 he was still a valued customer. We did some early work for Arthur Erickson before he became famous, for architect Frank Whitley, and Reed Jones Christofferson, Engineers.

It grew quite rapidly, I even made some money the first month and I had no bills to pay but I had to live so the money was welcome.

I stayed at that little office for a couple of years. There were other small offices in the building and I did work for some of them. There was a young fellow named Harold Petty, who was working for a company in eastern Canada and he wanted to go sailing around the world for a year. Eventually he did make the sailing trip with his family and visited us when he returned, to tell of his experiences.

Lloyd Muir kept me fairly busy when the racetrack was open, as well as at other times of the year. One of my least favourite tasks was to distribute posters promoting the racetrack to seedy third rate hotels. I was never comfortable doing this. Lloyd also did PR for some of the mining companies, so my field of contacts was expanding in more than one direction. He was the type of person who didn't do a lot of entertaining in the office but quite often would have people in for drinks after 5:00 and of course I was usually there working. I had the opportunity to meet quite a few people and tell them what I was doing. It was amazing to me that there was a real need for the type of services that Tri-C offered to big and small companies.

A lot of good contacts came through people I met through Mickey, who was with Pacific Western Airlines. We did brochures for them as well as other work. PWA had started in the early 50's, serving logging camps in northern communities, and had now become Canada's third major airline. They later bought Canadian Pacific and became the country's second largest airline.

Some of the PWA stewardesses, who wanted extra work, would come and work for me when they weren't flying. One of them married a man by the name of Harry Hole. His family owned the whaling station in Port Hardy where there was a lot of logging and fishing, as well as a tow boat business in Coal Harbour. They were friends of Mickey's and they too sent some business my way. It seemed that all these little tentacles went out and there was nearly always a response somewhere along the line. Tri-C was like Topsy - it just grew.

14

MICKEY MCGUIRE, DENIZE AND UNIDENTIFIED MAN LEAVING FOR A CONFERENCE IN TOFINO, CIRCA 1965 PHOTO: GRAPHIC INDUSTRIES

Who Did the Work?

Sandwell Engineering, which was a world wide company, was just a block or two from me and some of the girls who worked in their steno pool came to see me and said that they'd like to do extra work at night when I had some available. Gisela Breig had just come back from South America and came to me through my Sandwell connections. She came looking for part time work as she was not going to be able to work full time for a while. That's how she started and eventually she came to work for me full time - my first full time employee.

This was a time when working mothers were beginning to enter the workplace, in most cases part time. Many returned veterans were either still in school or just starting their careers and money was scarce. Often their wives would work part time in the evening. If Dad was at university he'd look after the kids for a few hours in the evening and Mom could work for me and not have to pay a sitter. Louise MacDonald worked part time as she and her husband had several children. They were saving money to move to Australia as they were very concerned that Russia was going to attack Vancouver. It was right in the midst of the Cold War then and there was a lot of speculation that Vancouver was going to be attacked.

Marie and Georgina, my partners, both had jobs. Marie Coffey was a girl from the US and she moved back and forth between Canada and the States. She'd stay here for six months or so and then she'd go back. Georgina Cantalini had been Mickey's secretary with the airline, and she stayed with them for quite some time, then she married a young employee from the airline and they stayed friends of mine for many years. Marie and Georgina worked nights in the beginning and then they both decided it really wasn't their thing – they didn't want to work full time plus evenings, so I was on my own with the Tri-C name.

Tri-C now required a staff and that's when Gisela began. Gisela became our editor, our proof-reader and a great support for me in all aspects of the business as we started our expansion into bigger and better things. Gisela had both good ideas and capabilities to implement these ideas for improvements, increased efficiency and service and always had input into any minor or major changes in company policy

My original concept for the company was to have clients come to us, rather than sending staff to their office. We provided the work space, equipment, paid the salaries and charged on an hourly basis ($2.50 an hour in the beginning). This way we had quality control, efficient staff and an on-going relationship with our clients. I never intended it to be more than a one or two person business.

Some of my nieces came to Vancouver for holidays in the summer and always came to work for a little while. They became my part time staff and at times their friends would come and help. Margo and Carol McGuire, Mickey's nieces, came to work in the summer because they had just moved here from Edmonton so I had lots of help to staple and collate and run the Gestetner (an early printing device). They worked for 75 cents an hour, so expenses were low. When they weren't around I would take a lot of work home. I was living at Point Grey and would take stapling and collating home and set my apartment up as a semi-work office. Mickey would come up there some nights, stapling and hammering and pounding – the neighbours couldn't figure out what was going on.

My niece, Hazel Wright, came to Vancouver in 1962 when she was about 20 to look for a job. She planned to stay with me so I put her to work right away as we were very busy at the time. She liked it so well that she stayed on, which meant that, with Gisela, there were now three of us full time and some part time staff as well. I now had my own Gestetner and we had switched to electric typewriters and electric adding machines. We also had contact with some good printers. If jobs couldn't be done by Gestetner then we'd send them out for printing.

Hazel stayed with me for over two years and actually ran the office a couple of times when I was away traveling in Europe. The first time it was for six weeks. Gisela was the senior girl but she didn't want to be in charge. So I said, "Well Hazel, I guess you're in charge." And she said, "OK, but I probably won't be able to do it." However she managed quite well.

Hazel Wright

An interesting story from that time shows how well she coped. We had a client who had a drinking problem. Some of the men who spent a lot of their lives traveling ended up this way. We had some problems from time to time because of his liking for alcohol and we knew his wife, because she would call sometimes trying to find him. While I was gone, this man had people visiting, went on a really bad spree of drinking, had a massive heart attack and died. He was missing for a few days before his body was discovered and during this period Hazel kept in touch with his family and did some things for them and then finally went to the funeral. She was one of those people who had a fear of dying and funerals were something she avoided if possible. When I came back I asked her, "Why did you go to the funeral?" She said, "Well, I know that if you'd been here you would have gone." She was a very strong support for me during those two years.

She was a very clever girl and had insurance experience, which was something I lacked, so she fit in very well. Hazel was very shy but she liked to get involved and was very teachable. She had known me her whole life and even though I was a bossy person she knew that I got things done. She also knew that if she wanted to work for me it had to be my way or the highway. We had that kind of relationship where I was the boss at the office but I was Auntie Dee at home. We lived together for the two years she worked for me, which was amazing. She was extremely good at taking over and taking instruction. If you told her what you wanted her to do you knew that she was listening and paying attention. She had been quite strictly brought up by my sister so there was a strong family connection.

Hazel finally decided to return to Edmonton and then her younger sister Shirley came to Vancouver after she graduated from university with a B.Ed. degree. She had worked for me in the summers while she attended university and had done a lot of specification work for architects. This became her specialty and soon she was dating a draftsman who worked for Mr. Whitley, one of our architectural clients. As Mr. Whitley's office became busier he offered Shirley a job and she went there with my blessing. I knew what the attraction was in their office and eventually Shirley married Larry Furneau, the draftsman she had been dating. Meanwhile Mr. Whitley continued to bring a lot of overload work to us. Nepotism in the above cases certainly paid off for me.

Any time I needed to hire someone I would let our customers know. At other times they would tell me about someone who was looking for work. As time went on we had contact with a large number of people throughout the city and staffing was never a problem. We didn't have a high turnover overall because most people came and stayed.

All of my employees had a reason for coming and because I was able to make the hours flexible I was able to get good help. There was tremendous response from everybody that worked for me. In 1971 Marlies McGuire (Mickey's daughter-in-law) began. She came in at 9:30 and worked 'til 2:30 so that she could be home when her children came home from school. Her bus would get her home about the same time they arrived from school and if she was needed at home in the morning she would always let me know in advance so we could re-arrange her hours. Our hours were secondary to the family hours and it worked well. It wasn't always convenient but there was usually somebody else around that could fill in.

Marlies began with us on Burrard Street, where new and enlarged premises gave us the opportunity to implement the idea of packaged offices. We had started this in a small way at Georgia Street but were now extending this idea in a more professional way. Marlies became official greeter, otherwise known as "The Receptionist". She was our main contact with all customers, receiving compliments and complaints with equal poise. She had numerous phones to answer – our first actual switchboard – and became very efficient at saying, "Please hold a moment, I'll be right with you", and went on to another client who was waiting. As our first contact with prospects, she was a great PR gal and usually intrigued most of them so that they made an appointment and nine times out of ten did become clients of Tri-C. Marlies and her family; Mickey, Stephen and Christine, could be called upon in any emergency for a few hours painting, repairs, stuffing envelopes or running the Gestetner.

I believe I was able to offer my employees varied hours of work because I didn't have any family commitments and had a 24 hour day that I personally controlled. If I had to stay until midnight or get up at 6:00 am to get something finished I did it. Because we had such a standardized format, different people could work on the same job and we kept everything as simple as possible, I was able to give my girls time off as they needed it. Because we were flexible everyone was willing to stay if it was necessary, and they would make special arrangements to do so. Then when they needed time off they didn't hesitate to ask for it. Our concept was "We are here to serve the public but our staff is important too." As business continued to increase and diversify so did our staff, and this enabled us to cover evenings and weekend work as required.

If someone came to me with a new idea I wasn't averse to trying it. We did talk about the business a good deal, especially when there were just three or four of us there. Gisela was very good; she was very well trained and she was never hesitant to suggest a new or better way to handle a problem.

Everybody in the office had to be flexible, but the one big disadvantage was that we never had a sufficient number of employees to qualify for benefits that larger companies could offer so there was no way to have medical and other benefits for the staff. We never did reach that stage.

Setting Standards

Once I got going I loved every day. There were a few challenges along the way but most people were so great to work with and I had the greatest staff, the most willing bunch of people working for me all the time and it was good. We set up a work code and each person had to be able to do any job we were working on. As we got bigger and busier one person could not always complete a large job and that meant that three people or more might have to work on one job and yet all the work had to look exactly the same (this was in the days of typewriters, long before computers). All the margins had to be the same, indenting had to be the same etc. We had a pattern for letters where they began at a certain line on the page, depending on the size of the letter, and yet sometimes something had to be done over because it didn't quite match. We used back-up sheets which set out all the specifications, and these helped to make all the work consistent.

It finally became such that I could get up from my typewriter and somebody else could sit down and continue and there wouldn't be any change in the finished look of the job. It was very important that we kept that up. We did all architectural specifications in the exact same manner, unless there was some reason not to – a mark at the bottom where you stopped, a mark at the top where you started – so many indents and paragraphs. It had to be standardized and there was pressure from me to do this. If anyone didn't do it there was no way they could stay but I fired very few people, only one or two in 28 years. Most of the girls that came to work liked it and stayed as long as possible.

There were lots of laughs and lots of fun and a few tears. There were very few times we had to say to a customer "Don't bother coming back". I did say that to a couple of them because they were unreasonable about whom they would talk to - if I wasn't there they wouldn't talk to anyone else – they would just have to see Denize. If they found out that Denize didn't do it, it wasn't right. Often they were quite rude. I remember one man in particular, when he came in I said, "I need to talk to you" and took him into an empty office so that no one would overhear. I explained to him that we didn't want to work for him any more because he didn't treat my employees with respect. He was unhappy and I explained that it had been going on for some time and I had mentioned to him before that we couldn't tolerate that attitude. He was really upset but he wasn't going to change so that was the end of it. I found only one or two people like that over the years.

We had some other difficult people but usually they came around. For instance there was one man who would sit and look at a letter until he found a mistake – sometimes it took him half an hour. Finally we learned that on his jobs we needed to leave one little mistake, which he pounced on with glee. We fixed it and he went away happy and we were happy too!!

Moving On and Up

Tri-C stayed in that first office for two years. At the end of the first year Lloyd went on to bigger and better offices and I took over his space. As soon as I installed my own phone it was the 681-0295 number, which is still in use today, but at that time it was Pacific 0295. By that time we were doing work for BC Industries, the company next door. They were one of the first importers to bring in merchandise from Japan and they had a small sales staff. Dominion Blueprint was part of their organization and there was work coming in from them as well.

When space came available in the building next door we moved there in 1959. I had business cards printed right away and chose blue, with matching letterhead and invoices. I still have a Tri-C tag on my traveling bag.

The new office was in one of those older buildings that had other small companies renting office space. I had already made contact with them and was doing work for all of them. John Beveridge was one tenant – he sold office furniture and had a small office but no staff and we took over his telephone answering and any other assistance he required. There was one telephone answering company in the city at that time but it was very impersonal. We also took over Canadian Titanium Pigment's telephone answering and secretarial duties. Then I had people coming in looking for desk space. There were three or four other offices available so we started supplying "desk" space. Dominion Blue and BC Industries had a staff but whenever they needed overload work done we handled it. There was an insurance company there, and when Hazel arrived with insurance experience she took over their work. We worked for everybody else who was in that little building.

Soon we were doing telephone answering for five or six companies in our building. We were in that building when John Kennedy was shot in November 1963, and were there until 1968. The building was being demolished and we had to find a new place for Tri-C and others who wished to move with us.

Mr. Alan Smith owned the building on Burrard Street where we eventually moved. John Beveridge was moving to the east side of Burrard and introduced us. It turned out that Alan had studied engineering at the University of Alberta with my brother Richard, who was killed overseas in World War II. When I got to know Alan and found the link with my brother he was always very good to me and was as helpful as he possibly could be. He used to want to take me out and buy me drinks at night but I didn't go very often. I liked to keep most of my relationships with my clients strictly business, and of course most of my social life was with Mickey. There was really very little temptation.

Once again in these new premises our business increased – new opportunities presented themselves. We hired new staff, upgraded our equipment and moved on to bigger adventures.

A Big Move

After ten years on Burrard Street it became necessary to move again when the building was to be demolished. Meanwhile we had run out of room, with seven offices rented plus our own space. There were now three of us in the office full time, plus several part time people.

We also made use of a government program which subsidized students who needed summer work; from both university and high schools. In return for the subsidy we gave them instruction and supervision and then finally reported on their progress. We first began using this program in the early '70s and I believe we were one of the first companies to do so. Each year we would hire one or two students because Marlies needed the summer off to be with her children and every second year Gisela spent two months in Europe. The program was valuable for us and I believe that it was valuable for the young women who came to work for us.

When I decided to move Tri-C to 1250 Homer the Atkins brothers, owners of the building, thought I was taking on something that I wouldn't be able to handle. They were skeptical that this little Tri-C company could take over 5,400 square feet and manage to pay the rent. I had been looking for suitable space and when I saw this building it looked promising. Soon I was face to face with Don and Brian Atkins at their office, which was just a block down Homer street. Don in particular was concerned to see me moving from a relatively small space to take over a whole floor of their building. He said, "Maybe you'd be better to take half the space." I said, "No, I want it all and I'll redecorate it." He was really concerned that I was jumping into something that was way, way too big for me, and so they gave me a break on the rent for the first year, which was very helpful because I had a lot of work to do there.

The building was just a warehouse and the first floor had a few offices along one side. Jack Blachford, a space planner and one of our clients, gave me some suggestions, one of which was to hire an interior decorator. His vision was great but over my budget, and I couldn't afford to follow all of his suggestions. Finally I told him that I was going to have to do it myself. First of all I had a carpenter come in and partition a dozen offices to make a total of 16 altogether. Then I had some friends help with the painting on a voluntary basis but they weren't making much progress, so I spoke with another friend in Surrey who was a professional painter. He said that he could come and paint the whole floor in a week or 10 days, so I fired my volunteers and brought in a professional. They did a very simple job and made it look clean and tidy. Finally I had the floor covered with carpet and that finished what was a really big, major undertaking. We blocked off the back half at first because we didn't yet have furniture for those offices.

At Burrard Street we had seven offices, so now our rentable space was more than doubling, plus our work space was tripled. I felt it was one of those moves I was forced to make because you can't stand still. A challenge comes along and you have to go, or go out. A lot of people said that it was too much but I said, "Well, I'll go with it and hope it works out reasonably well." And it did. Tri-C was on a roll again.

Marketing the Offices

We had taken on SME (Sales & Marketing Executives) as a client just before the move, and a number of their members came in as tenants. Many of them were young entrepreneurs starting out on their own. Often they worked from home at first and then realized that they needed to have an office and found that our furnished space was very affordable. They simply arranged to have a phone installed and they were in business, with a receptionist, telephone answering, plus access to telex (a precursor to the fax) and photocopiers. And they had no payroll, they simply paid Tri-C at the end of the month for any work we had done, such as typing letters. And of course each of these SME members had a number of friends and they spread the word on our behalf.

I never did any advertising; people came in as a result of the organizations we were working for or word of mouth from our clients. I think we may have sent out a little mailing to the people in our vicinity after we moved in, to let them know we were there. I still did some calls but not a lot. We had a fairly big sign on the side of the building facing traffic, because in those days Homer Street was one way. It said:

Tri-C Secretarial Services
Offices for Rent
Telephone Answering

An asset at that location was the large parking lot adjacent to the building. It was used by our staff, tenants and other clients.

My Business Philosophy

Each move gave me the same feeling – I really don't want to move, I'm quite happy here, I don't want to get any bigger, I don't want to do this, I don't want this business to grow. And then to move in and figure out how we could fit everybody into the space – each move was big. Luckily they were all in the west end and I didn't have too far to walk to work. Each move improved the quality of service we could give and was an upgrading; we had more space, nicer space, new business cards, more staff, more phones. Each move was good - it just seemed to come with the move. And each time we moved we had a whole new area in which to market our services.

There was a time when John Beveridge moved to a new location and one of our Tri-C girls would go over to his office twice a week. Eventually he hired her full time. Most companies wouldn't have allowed it but to me if she wanted to go and work there she wouldn't do any good working for me.

Tri-C was a tremendous experience and I had a great staff, but I don't think I could survive now – they don't do things the way we used to. I said this to some of the girls I know, "Boy, you sure wouldn't have lasted with me for very long with your attitude. We treated our customers with respect." I don't know if it's just the generation gap but there's no way that I could survive a month in the workforce today. I'd be totally frustrated. People seem to be under so much stress today.

I seldom pick up a book or an article that I don't find misused words, either used in the wrong context or misspelled. The computer will not always do the right thing – words are split anywhere, there is no sense of where you're supposed to split a word. Then you get the words that we never would have broken up – it would have been totally unacceptable. Also there are so many new words in the English language, like "wellness" for one. There never was a word called "wellness". You were well or you were ill, but you weren't partially well or you didn't have a wellness feeling. I dislike that word and yet everybody uses it and it's in the dictionary now. And I sometimes look at something and think, "Oh, I wish Gisela had read this and edited it before these people printed it. She was absolutely great, she could take something and pick up all the mistakes and yet English wasn't her first language. She knew the right words to use."

Most of the people that we worked for were household names, like Noma Lites. I always felt that we were doing good work for them and becoming part of something bigger than just Tri-C. We were able to drop names more than occasionally. I still find that when I listen to the news and read newspapers and see people in the news, in trouble and otherwise, I can look back and say, "I remember working with that particular person or I remember that company." This brought the whole world into our office in many ways.

As I grew up, because things were difficult we were encouraged that if we wanted something we had to work for it. It was the way of life in those days. If you didn't work you didn't eat. You didn't have any recreation, you made your own. I think that young people today miss so much, growing up with little discipline in their lives. They need things, they want things and they don't learn that they appreciate things so much more if they have worked for them.

Looking for a Partner

Along with this major expansion I began to think about finding a partner who would eventually take over the business. I had talked to a number of employees to see whether there was any interest, but none of the women who had worked for me had been interested in taking on the responsibility. I didn't use a lot of consultants in those days because I had worked with so many people and gained information from so many sources that it wasn't necessary. Now I had a good general knowledge of how I wanted to go about it.

It seemed that bringing in a partner and having shares gradually acquired was the preferred method of handing over the company.

Don Cameron was the company accountant, knew the business quite well, and he did have some input on what would be a reasonable value for the business. He gave me some good advice about how we should operate the partnership. He advised that it shouldn't be a long lasting one as there would eventually be a conflict of interest because the other person would want to get in and I'd still be the boss and he suggested it be as short as possible, which turned out to be pretty good advice I think.

It is hard to be a half boss and a half worker on either side of the fence.

When I told Don what I planned to do he came up with some working plans to get a partnership rolling. He did the calculations of the value and he knew what it had been producing over the years and where it could go in the future. He was a very good person to have involved; he was reliable, professional and just a good man.

Now all that was necessary was to find a suitable candidate. I never advertised for people to work for me, I just picked people up off the street. I think the Good Lord was in charge; he'd send people to me who were looking for work.

Chapter Three
BERNICE JOINS DENIZE

Bernice is Job Hunting

*I*t was early February of 1978 and I had recently arrived in Vancouver with my 16-year-old daughter Annette. This was my second attempt to leave a troubled marriage and I was determined not to go back this time.

My oldest son, Lance DeCaire, serviced photocopiers with Pitney Bowes and one evening he dropped in to see how my job hunt was going. We were living in a furnished apartment but couldn't have a phone installed because the telephone company was on strike. This made communication with prospective employers difficult so I had done most of my job hunting through personnel agencies. My dream was to find a job in a large company with lots of benefits so that I could have Annette's teeth straightened, but after three weeks I was coming up empty handed. Also, my money had run out and I'd had to borrow from my brother so it was really important to find a job right away.

Lance suggested I try a small office on Burrard Street. He had been servicing their copier that day and said that they always seemed busy and right now appeared to be short handed.

Early the next day I arrived at the office he had suggested and was directed to Denize Callaway. She didn't have a lot of time to interview me, but asked a few questions and then gave me a letter to type. When it was finished she looked it over and said, "Do you want to stay and work now, or come back tomorrow morning?" I decided to come back tomorrow as I liked to have something new to wear to a new job. As I looked around the small office I knew this wasn't my dream job, yet it was what I needed just now. It was important to get established in Vancouver. I'd spent too many years in small towns and this was exactly where I wanted to be.

First priority was shopping for shoes. Next I left a message for Lance to come and see me after work. He and Annette and I had a happy little celebration that evening.

Next morning I arrived at Tri-C Secretarial Services Ltd. in my new shoes and spent a most productive day. There was not much time for orientation. Tri-C was moving March 31 to 1250 Homer Street and this was why the office was short staffed these days. Denize was often at the new location, supervising painters and carpet layers and taking delivery of new furniture.

Meanwhile I met our in-house clients and found my new co-workers, Gisela and Marlies, most helpful and efficient. And now I learned to work harder than I ever had in my life! By Friday night every week I was exhausted – the variety of people we served and the complexity of the work took all of my energy to encompass. Additionally there were templates for every job, letters had to be typed in a certain format and the envelopes had to be typed in a certain format. Often more than one person worked on a job and templates ensured that the change would be seamless.

Then I was given a sheet on which time was tracked by the quarter hour – every quarter hour of the whole work day! As a new employee, if it took me a half hour to type a one page letter instead of the standard quarter hour, I charged the client a quarter hour and the company for the other quarter. No one was overcharged and I quickly learned how fast I had to work. I could also see how much unproductive time had accumulated by the end of the day and I was determined to make every hour count as soon as possible.

Moving to Yaletown

March 31st soon arrived and we were now in much larger quarters, over 5,000 square feet, and the entire first floor of a building with 16 offices around the periphery at 1250 Homer Street. We staff members worked at the front half of the central area. An interesting feature was a huge walk-in safe (actually a room), which made a perfect place to store paper documents (both our own and clients) where they would be safe from fire. We were now in "Yaletown", one of the oldest areas of the city, soon to become the trendiest, with a big loading dock at the rear and a huge freight elevator just inside the back of the building. In the basement was a company doing bulk mailing; a service we soon found useful.

In 1978 Yaletown was still very much a warehouse area and the closest restaurant was three blocks away on Granville Street. There was no time to go out for lunch so we all brought a sandwich and gathered around Denize's desk for a half hour. The coffee pot was always on and we helped ourselves but never took a formal coffee break. In the new office there was a new rule – no smoking at your desk – the ashtray was beside the coffee pot, out of sight of the reception area.

GISELA, BERNICE AND MARLIES AT 1250 HOMER STREET

Marlies was receptionist and did telephone answering. I sat behind her and Denize trained me to handle work intake from outside clients. Gisela handled the telex machine and the postage meter. Denize spent much of her time on administration for Sales and Marketing Executives and the rest on Tri-C management. Just now that meant marketing the empty offices (only half were filled when we first moved in). And, along with these main duties we all typed.

Our First Computer

We were just nicely settled when Don Thomas, an architectural specification writer, began campaigning for a word processing machine. This would allow him to modify previous specs, which would be stored electronically. At that time he was paying us to type dozens of pages for each specification, and he knew there was a better way. It was a huge investment for a small company but Don was a good client and Denize and Gisela checked out what was available and settled on a Xerox 850 dedicated word processor, which had a full screen display and a Diablo printer. The cost of that machine in 1979 was more than ten times what the company would pay in 2007 for one computer and printer.

GISELA WITH FULL PAGE DISPLAY WORD PROCESSOR, 1979

Gisela had requested to become the machine operator and off she went to a three-day training course. She would come in at the end of each day completely drained and I knew it was a difficult task for her. She feared she would become outdated if she didn't learn, and as she was a single mother, the sole support of her son Ingo, it was necessary that she remain well skilled. A few months later I took the course so that I could do back-up for Gisela when she visited Germany during July and August on alternate years. The training was less stressful for me because I had lots of time to do fill-in work before Gisela left and the workload was lighter in July and August when she was away. Also, I had experience on an electronic typewriter, which was like a word processor without a screen.

Happy Times

We all worked very hard but there were lighter moments. "Smokey" Smith would come in to make photocopies for the travel agency run by his wife. He was a jolly man who loved to chat and each year gave us a report on his visit to Buckingham Palace, where he was honoured as one of Canada's holders of the Victoria Cross, the highest military honour in both Britain and Canada. In later years he took his grandchildren in turn and it must have been a wonderful trip for each of them.

SMOKEY SMITH AND DENIZE

Paul Binkley was a client who had both a great sense of humour and excellent story-telling capability. We laughed 'til we cried when he told us about his one and only experience making egg salad sandwiches.

He wasn't aware that egg salad sandwiches contained mayonnaise to hold the bits of egg together, however he remembered seeing someone mash up the eggs so he did that. Then he buttered the bread and began to pile the egg on the bread. The egg kept rolling off of course, but he persevered and finally pressed another slice of bread down on top of the egg and quickly wrapped up the sandwiches, as he was taking them to a party. The poor hostess had egg all over the floor before the party was over and Paul had many helpful females offering to assist the next time he made sandwiches for a party.

Another priceless story was the Vancouver to Maui Yacht Race. Paul was at a New Year's Eve party when someone asked for crew volunteers for the race. Paul said he would like to go but was dismayed once they were on board to find that many of the volunteers had no experience yachting in the Pacific Ocean. Several came along for the ride with no intention of working, while others were sick the whole way. He finally slid down the wall and sat on the floor, curled up in the fetal position, saying, "Can you imagine spending two weeks in a confined space with people you didn't know or like?" Paul had a marvelous ability to take us to another time and place and describe his feelings as he told the story.

Four Becomes Five

When Irene Doerksen came to us, we didn't know we needed someone that desperately but we knew we always needed some extra help. Carson Whyte of Westhawk Traders, came to our rescue. He knew Irene through his business connections in Manitoba, and when she spoke about moving to Vancouver he told her about Tri-C and suggested that she drop into his office and he would introduce her. Irene arrived, teeming with energy and high expectations of her move to the west coast. Surprise, surprise, we all thought we were great typists – fast and accurate – but Irene put us all to shame. She could out-type all of us and read bad handwriting as well.

IRENE DOERKSEN RELAXING WITH COFFEE

Denize said that she never advertised for help. We were very fortunate over all those years in the good people that came our way.

Denize as Mentor

VALERIE WATCHING DENIZE SPEAK, 1984

Denize trained her staff to be quick and accurate and to provide good customer service (not always an easy combination), however, her talent for "bringing people along" reached beyond her own staff. When she saw a capable person, like Valerie Jenkinson, she encouraged her to take the SME three year diploma course in Sales & Marketing Management at

UBC. Valerie did take the course and was the top grad in her year. We did the registration for both this course and also for the 12 week Vansec Sales Course. Because she saw the benefits of the courses Denize encouraged young SME members to take advantage of the training. With Valerie she also encouraged her to become involved on the executive and told her that she would be president some day. Valerie did become president, just the second woman to do so, and in 2005 she was a candidate for Vancouver City Council. She didn't make it the first time but I'm betting that she will next time.

Valerie remembers Denize as "calm in the midst of chaos". She describes Denize as the person who knew everything but did not "take charge". Instead she made other people look good. She also sees Denize as someone who was able to hire good people and train them well.

Denize Takes Me to Dinner

Near the time of my first anniversary Denize asked if I'd like to have dinner with her. Most of her conversation usually centred on the business and I wasn't surprised when the same was true that evening. I was however very surprised when she asked if I'd like to become a partner. Because I was always looking for a good opportunity elsewhere I had never looked at my present position as having any potential, and didn't realize that she was planning to retire. I told her that I would consider it but not to expect an answer quickly.

From that day on I looked at the business from a different perspective. I soon realized that we did well whether the economy was up or down. When times were good there was lots of work for everyone, and when things took a downturn companies laid off staff and brought their overload work to us. I began to see the possibilities but had no money, only a one thousand dollar RRSP.

Timeout for some background on my finances and why I had the RRSP. When I left my husband I took an assumed name so that he couldn't find me. This meant that I had no credit record and when Christmas came that first year I had difficulty shopping without a credit card. This was long before there were ATM machines. I knew that it was important to establish a credit record, so in early 1979 I approached the bank for a loan of $1,000 to purchase an RRSP. This was not a risk for the bank as they kept the money.

I made regular payments on the loan and a few months later applied for a credit card. They issued me a card with a small limit and again I made regular payments, however I didn't believe that the bank would lend me the amount I needed to put a down payment on the business - that was a whole different ball game. I did realize the value of my credit record and each month my bills were paid on time. Meanwhile Denize didn't even ask me whether I was still interested – there was absolutely no pressure from her.

It was almost a year after our dinner that my parents came to visit and at some point my father said that he had just sold two houses in Markham. That triggered an idea and finally I asked whether he would lend me some money for a down payment on the business. He asked me a few questions and we discussed the possibilities, then without hesitation said that he would be happy to loan me the money. This didn't surprise me because he often told me when I was a young girl that he'd like me to be a teacher so that I could be self sufficient if anything ever happened to my husband. So now he was helping me to become self sufficient.

Before Mom and Dad left I spoke with Denize to make sure that the opportunity was still there and we settled the deal. Actually Dad lent me half of the down payment and I went to the bank to borrow the other half. The loan from my Dad was put in writing and I was to send him a monthly cheque to pay the 10% interest on the loan, with the principal to be repaid after I took full control of the company. Interest rates were high at the time and the loan from my father was a bargain at 10%, while the bank loan was considerably higher.

The Contract

The company accountant, Don Cameron, wrote a buy sell agreement for us. He also suggested that we each set up a holding company to transfer the shares. This was all good experience for me as I learned how to register a company. It also gave me a vehicle to document the interest payments I was making to my Dad and the bank. The advantage was that I paid almost no income tax during the time I was buying shares in the business.

Don also suggested that Denize and I buy life insurance on each other so that if one of us died the other would have the money to buy the remaining shares from our heirs. It was 1980 when I became a partner at Tri-C with the purchase of thirty percent of the shares. The agreement set out that I would gradually purchase the remainder of the shares over the next four years.

Changes I Made as a Partner

First of all was finance. Most months it took two to three weeks to issue invoices for the services rendered. The process was lengthy and time consuming and Denize would take home the time sheets because there was no time in the workday to handle them. Labour for each client was accumulated on a work sheet; taking hours from each employee's daily time sheet (it was not unusual for each person's daily sheet to have 15 – 20 entries). Then other charges were added such as rent, photocopies, postage, faxes etc. Everything was added up and sales tax added to taxable items. Finally invoices were typed, taking all information from the work sheets. It is difficult to imagine now what an onerous task this was but I volunteered to take it on and set a goal to have them completed by the third day of each month. This had a significant impact on our cash flow.

Denize had little time to make collection calls for outstanding accounts so I took this on as well. I could soon see why she needed a partner. Regular phone calls improved our collection rate. Customers who were walk-ins (as compared to in-house) were often given credit without making any credit inquiries. As I was taking in the work I began to ask that we be paid when the work was picked up rather than letting people charge. This way I got to know them before we offered credit terms and again it bumped up our cash flow and saved time chasing laggards.

One thing that didn't need changing was the attitude to work. One day I heard Don Thomas, who worked alone at home, remark to Denize, "Wow, the vibes in this place – you are all strong, hard-working women and there is so much energy here!" One of the women from the Western Businesswomen's Association told me later that they were in awe of us and really admired our concept of providing services to both individuals and organizations.

Self Development

I learned about the Vansec Sales Course by attending SME meetings with Denize and found the course appealing. In Vansec we were taught to set goals, how to sell services to a prospective client, and most importantly, how to overcome fear of the unknown. Mid way in the course we had to write ourselves a congratulatory letter on completing something we'd always wanted to do but feared to do. Our instructor, Laurence Lovett, collected the letters which were sealed in self addressed envelopes with the date for mailing written in the top right corner where it would be covered by the stamp. As the date approached I still hadn't found the courage to take the parachute jump I'd promised myself. I thought perhaps something a little safer would do and went for a ride on the roller coaster at Exhibition Park, but that didn't work for one minute! The letter arrived at the appointed time but I didn't open it because I had yet to earn it.

BERNICE IN JUMP SUIT, READY TO GO, SEPTEMBER 9, 1979

The course began in January, I wrote the letter in March and it was mailed to me in June. It wasn't until late August that I psyched myself up to proceed. I went to Horizon Aerosports on Kingsway with cash in hand (they didn't accept cheques or charge cards) and found the office closed for lunch. I walked up and down the street, waiting for someone to return, asking myself "Is this an omen that I shouldn't go?" I was soon signed up for Sunday September 9th, and now it was official. And once I'd paid my money I knew I'd do it. This was definitely the best goal-setting technique I've ever seen. Gisela came along to take pictures. Annette didn't want to watch and my mother didn't want to know when I was jumping, but Gisela knew how important it was to me. The day after the parachute jump, as I walked to work people kept smiling at me and I wondered why. Then it occurred to me that I must have a big smile on my face. I thought then that I'd never again be afraid to do anything, however the reality is that I'm still afraid sometimes, but don't let that stop me from moving ahead.

In the sales course I learned that I had little confidence doing presentations and knew that further training was needed. I found that a Toastmistress Club (a female version of Toastmasters) met two Monday evenings a month just a few blocks from the office. The organization was very like Toastmasters but with two focuses; speech training and organization structure (the latter became very valuable information as time went on). We met for dinner and learned to speak both off the cuff and from prepared material. Constant evaluation improved our skills (both speaking and analytical). The first time I spoke in front of 100 people it was a huge accomplishment. In a short time I was president of the club and this gave me an opportunity to practice leadership skills.

I took many courses to prepare to take over the business but had most difficulty in learning how to produce financial statements. They were always a mystery to me. Two different courses left me confused and it wasn't until Neil McLeod (an accountant and the new man in my life at the time) found me a workbook which began with the balance sheet, that I finally understood the process. This was a huge accomplishment and left me feeling powerful. It was almost as difficult as learning to live without cigarettes.

Trade Organizations

I found such groups to be of immense value, mostly for the opportunity to exchange ideas with other people and sometimes work on common problems. In most cases family and friends aren't as likely to have the kind of expertise and understanding as another business person.

Canadian Office Services Organization (COSA) was a local group of people with similar businesses; some packaged offices and some secretarial services. Members were willing to share their expertise and we often referred prospects we couldn't help to another member. Sometimes a phone call to someone with an educated ear was all that we needed to solve a problem. I also was privileged to be elected president of this group, another opportunity to hone my management skills.

The National Association of Secretarial Services (NASS) was headquartered in Florida with members all over North America. This was where I learned about Industry standards (much like those we already used in our office) and learned about new developments in the field of secretarial services. NASS in later years did a feature article on me in their newsletter.

GROUP OF FIVE, L-R STAN, JOYANNA, BERNICE, RANDY, RALPH, 1997

The Group of Five was an informal group which was without a name in the beginning. Joyanna Anthony gathered four other people including Ralph Johnstone, Stan Shackell, Randy Singer and myself to meet for breakfast one Saturday morning each month. We all lived on the North Shore and ran our own businesses. At each session we each had a half hour to talk about problems or plans for our own company and ask the others for feedback. If we came back too often with the same problem there was a lot of kidding, but also lots of good input. It took a while to build a level of trust but eventually a strong bond developed and I wouldn't miss our breakfasts for anything.

Building Association Business

While I was in the throes of self development Denize was busy building the business. She had filled all the offices before I became a partner, and her philosophy of providing excellent, time-efficient service brought many referrals from current clients.

Sales and Marketing Executives (SME) had become a client when the company was still on Burrard Street and was the first major association to become a client.

Irene Croden was a member of SME and she brought us the Western Businesswomen's Association (WBA) in 1979. She had been running the group out of her office for several years on a voluntary basis and now that she was leaving the board, wanted it to be in good hands.

A couple of years later Sally Rycroft of the WBA brought us the Canadian Association of Financial Planners (CAFP) which in time became our biggest association client and another source of expertise for me. One of their members became my personal financial planner, an excellent resource for any small business owner.

Canadian Information Processing Society (CIPS) came to ask us whether we could manage them. Because Irene had the most interest in computers she willingly took charge of their needs. They grew to be our largest client at a certain stage and of course they gave us insight into new developments in the data processing field.

Our landlords, Don and Brian Atkins, recommended us to take over the Canadian Club of Vancouver when their full time staff member died suddenly in 1982. (These are the same landlords who had initially doubted whether Tri-C could survive in this large space.) This was a much larger group than any we had at the time, with 1,400 members. Their board consisted of many high profile people in the business community and the prospect was daunting, especially considering that they held luncheons where the speakers included prime ministers and royalty. Denize suggested that I take responsibility for the Canadian Club and I did so with trepidation. They had two lunches each month and for the first few months I could not sleep on the night before these events.

BERNICE LEADING IN HEAD TABLE AT FIRST EVENT WE MANAGED FOR THE CANADIAN CLUB AT HOTEL VANCOUVER (SPEAKER WAS EDITOR OF THE GLOBE & MAIL) 1982. CP AIR PHOTO

The Atkins brothers also suggested we assist a group new to Vancouver called Crime Stoppers. They needed a telephone answering service and had no money, so we provided the service on a voluntary basis, using our second telephone line (681-0296). For many years we gave the same service to Toastmasters for a very small fee. I believed so much in their great training program that I felt they deserved the support. This latter continued for many years until they set up a website, however Crime Stoppers was with us for just two years until they were able to set up their own office.

Part Time Employees

Diana Gray comes to mind as a highly capable young woman who worked in the evenings in addition to her day job at Vancouver School Board. She was new to Vancouver and looking for opportunities. Before long she was in business on Broadway as "My Private Secretary", and later established herself in Burnaby as "Central Park Business Centre". We often sent business her way when we were overloaded because we knew that she was highly capable and that her customers would receive excellent service.

Just as Denize enjoyed hiring her nieces I found it fun to bring in my young grandchildren, Shana, Amber and Roddy George, to stuff envelopes when they visited from Prince George. Later when I sold the business Shana said, "But where will Jenna (her daughter) find her first job?"

As our work was gradually computerized the need for extra hands lessened. The evolution of electronic communication is a good example. In 1980 we were still using a telex, which sent a printed message over a telephone line. Next came the fax machine, which would send both text and pictures over a telephone line. The broadcast fax was the next step whereby the same message could be sent over a phone line to many people and could be set to send at night when phone lines were not busy. Fast-forward to broadcast email which doesn't require a phone line and allows us to send the same message to hundreds or thousands of people instantly.

No longer is it necessary to type 90 words a minute. It is more important to know how to use the many computer programs in addition to word processing; database, spreadsheets and accounting just to cover the basics. Two qualities that are still necessary are intelligence and common sense. With these qualities an employee can be trained to use programs, to organize their work efficiently and most importantly, to provide good customer service.

Summing up the Partnership

The four years of our partnership from 1980 to 1984 went quickly at first, then more slowly in the last year as I became eager to take over. Little did I realize there would be a rocky road ahead once Denize was gone. It was a little like childbirth; if you knew what was ahead you might decide not to go there, but once you got through the tough times it was a lot of fun.

In the summer of 1984 Pope John Paul II visited Vancouver and Denize was heavily involved in plans to organize his visit. That was also the summer that my father had both his legs amputated, however I was unable to go to Toronto to be with my parents as I had to run the business. Denize had indicated that she would leave at the end of October so with the help of Neil McLeod I spent many hours on summer week-ends listing and marking every piece of furniture and equipment in 16 offices, five secretarial stations and four cubicles. This list, complete with approximate selling values, became part of the final sale document.

Up to this point we had managed without a lawyer as we depended on the company accountant, Don Cameron, to organize our contract. Meanwhile he had left his company and another partner, Ron Vonk, took over our account. I found the final document restrictive and did visit a lawyer, who assured me that it was indeed fair as Denize still had a financial interest but wouldn't be involved at all in running the business. I determined at this point that I would acquire the last few shares as quickly as possible so that my actions wouldn't be restricted by having to ask permission for major decisions.

Once the legal issues were worked out it was time to plan a celebration. We had a good template to work from as we had held a Christmas Open House every year for the past six years. We did plan it as a surprise for Denize and invited as many former clients as we could find.

DENIZE AND MICKEY MCGUIRE

We were accustomed to making food at home and bringing it to the party, however for this event my youngest son Dale was in town. He is a chef and with one helper organized a wonderful buffet with the piece de resistance a checker-board of light and dark caviar. I was very proud of him that evening.

FOOD AT PARTY WITH CHEF DALE DECAIRE AND HELPER

DENIZE AND GISELA CUTTING CAKE, AFTER MORE THAN 20 YEARS WORKING TOGETHER

Many people came that evening to honour Denize and her accomplishments over more than 27 years. She had brought Tri-C from a one woman operation in bartered office space to a five woman operation in more than 5,000 square feet, complete with furnished offices. During that time Tri-C had become THE place to go for good secretarial service in Vancouver, whether you were a small business person or a non-profit society.

DENIZE AND FLOWERS AT HER RETIREMENT PARTY, 1984

Just prior to our party SME had honoured Denize at one of their dinners, where her considerable contribution to the organization was recognized. Gisela, Marlies, Irene and I were all invited to attend that evening. Denize had brought stability and good organizational skills to a group whose strength lay in marketing. Once they had a solid base the board members were able to use their considerable talents to expand the group and it became one of the strongest SME chapters. That night letters were read from all over North America, praising Denize's contribution to SME. George Dedrick, 1976-77 president, pointed out that SME-Vancouver left its mother organization, the Vancouver Board of Trade in 1972 to go on their own, saying it proved to be a right decision "because of a super lady who provided us with office space and secretarial service. From that moment onward, SME hasn't looked back." At the end of the program Denize was presented with an honorary membership while the audience gave her a standing ovation.

TERESA EVANS, EDITOR OF THE MARKETER
PHOTO BY TOR BENGTSON

We were very proud of Denize that evening and it was all reported in "The Marketer", edited by Teresa Evans. This was SME's monthly newsletter and I never saw a better chapter publication than the one she produced.

Chapter Four
DENIZE REMEMBERS SOME INTERESTING CLIENTS

*W*e had worked for the Serra Club, a men's club, before we moved to Burrard Street. I didn't make that contact through the Catholic Church but when they came to see me and found I was Catholic and would understand some of the work they were doing, that was an advantage for them. Over the years we did a fair amount of work for the Church. Father LaSalles wrote a book about the native people in North Vancouver and Gisela typed pretty well all of his manuscript. That was when we were on Burrard Street and his book is still in print and highly regarded by those in government who are working with First Nations people.

We did most of the specifications for Simon Fraser University, under the direction of Arthur Erickson and Geoffrey Massey. We did all the specifications for TRIUMF at the University of British Columbia. Montreal Engineering was in charge and we did all the work for them in Vancouver for many years. David Duguid was in charge and they did work in northern BC and in the Yukon and we were involved in that as well. There was a lot of development going on in those days and of course we didn't say much about who we were working for, but other people would meet someone in the office and ask if we were doing work for them. We would say yes we do but never discussed what we were doing – that was confidential.

Gordon Minchin used to drive us crazy but he was a really interesting person to work for. When you finally finished what he wanted he was very happy and he never complained that you had to re-do and re-do because it was always his changes. After our first word processor arrived I said to Gisela, "If we'd only had this when Mr. Minchin was here, look at the paper we could have saved, we would have just deleted and added to." We used to cut and paste and try to fit six letters into a five letter space. He always dressed very well and carried himself well and I have never met anyone with a better memory than he had. He could be dictating a letter and would give me people's phone numbers and there was never a mistake. And he would say to me, "You can reach so-and-so in England", and give me their phone number. I never saw a man with such a memory for detail, and yet we would do a letter and it would be perfect and he would sign it and then sit down and come back with marks through the whole letter and it would have to be done again. And he might do this three times, because he decided he hadn't said quite what he wanted to say. He didn't like dictating very much, he'd rather write. He was a very brilliant man with a high level of energy.

About 1960 airlines were beginning chartered flights and one of our clients became one of the first companies to offer air travel insurance. If you booked on a charter flight and couldn't go you were out your money; there was no possibility of changing your flight. There was another company who set up flight insurance directly for those traveling on PWA. Here again we were involved in companies with new concepts and it was exciting to watch how they progressed.

We also did reservations for the first Grand Opening of Whistler in 1966, at a time when the population was approximately 25 people. Intrawest was the company that later developed the townsite. Before they opened an office in Vancouver they set up a telephone in our office and we answered it on their behalf. For their first promotion we mailed thousands of brochures across Canada and the U.S. about this big new ski facility in Whistler. We took reservations and Gisela and I went up to Whistler to see the accommodations and village plans at an early stage. For the grand opening there were plane loads of passengers coming and it was almost a total disaster because there were no facilities in place. Whistler had neither restaurants nor hotels. Some of the people were booked into the Pemberton Hotel and we ended up taking a lot of calls from some unhappy people. During this period time sharing was a new concept and this was the basis for building many of the hotels in Whistler. At the same time Mickey and I bought the property in Pemberton, where I still live today.

Pat Canning was an unusual and brilliant woman. She worked to help underprivileged people by setting up co-op housing for them. Pat first came to us on Burrard Street as a referral from Ruth Ann Irving, who drafted the Strata Title Act. She was always applying for government grants and she knew who to go to for information and was quite a political person on her own. Pat was involved in some early co-op apartments that she had built in East Vancouver, which are still housing families on low incomes today. One was the first infill project in Vancouver and another was a combination strata/co-op project on leased land. They were good family homes for extended families, seniors, single mothers and ordinary working people. These people never owned the apartments but it was a decent place to live and it was affordable for them.

In 1968 the co-ops of Vancouver became a world wide model of effective use of land in cities. They were built under Section 56.1 of the National Housing Act, but in the mid-90's the federal government cancelled the program. The co-ops have been able to continue because of iron-clad agreements which are still in place.

ANNETTE AND CARSON LISTENING TO BRAD HOLMES

Brad Holmes was with Hunter Douglas Blinds and rented a large office. Brad was a tall, dark and handsome man who was utterly charming, yet he could be very tough. Early one morning I heard him on the phone to someone and I could hardly believe it was the same Brad who was always affable and considerate of the staff. We were all excited when he married a beautiful woman and they soon had children; however Brad died of cancer while still a young man.

Noma Lites had two rooms with us at 1250 Homer; one was a display area and the other an office. They were the largest Christmas lighting company in the world until they quit manufacturing in 1968. Herb Rideout was sales manager and he had several sales people. They were always good to us at Christmas and we were each invited to pick something from their display, which meant that over the years we were all well stocked with Christmas lights and decorations.

Bert Robinson was a salesman for one of our tenants and a very personable older man. He teased us a lot when he found out that we preferred to be called "women" rather than "girls". At Christmas he always brought in a card to "the wimmen of Tri-C" and even after he retired he continued to send us a card each Christmas. When he retired Bert was among a group of seniors who bicycled across Canada as part of a kinesiology experiment by Simon Fraser University. Some of us would like to have gone along but the Boss wouldn't give us the summer off!!

John Ketteringham, a salesman for Perkins Papers, was another tenant who was generous at Christmas. Each year Perkins made up big packages of special Christmas napkins and paper tablecloths and John would present one to each staff member.

JOHN KETTERINGHAM TENDING THE BAR

DENIZE WITH CARSON WHYTE OF WESTHAWK TRADERS AND SON GARY

Carson Whyte had an office with us on Burrard Street, as well as at 1250 Homer. Carson was popular with all of us. He shipped livestock feed from Manitoba to dealers in British Columbia and was a most patient and thoughtful man. One product that Carson introduced was Dignity Cat Litter and Valerie Jenkinson worked with him to promote the product. It didn't become big in North America, however it was used in Buckingham Palace. Later his son Gary worked with him and we found Gary just as good to work with as his dad. Carson died a few years ago and his loss was deeply mourned by all of us. He was a good friend and booster for Tri-C.

DIANE WATERS, IRENE CRODEN WITH MARLIES

Croden Waters was a placement agency that moved into the front office at 1250 Homer. The partners were Irene Croden and Diane Waters and they were two high energy women. They loved to celebrate their successes and once in a while we would hear a big "whoop" and a lot of laughter and know that they had just placed a client. Irene and Diane drove matching Mustang convertibles and their parking spaces were adjacent. Irene parked on the left and Diane on the right and each had their surnames on their license plates. Anyone driving by would read their company name, 'Croden Waters.'

Pfizer had a sales office with us. Their sales manager, Ken Pask, managed a group of six salespeople who covered British Columbia. Bernice tells me that Ken advised her one day to buy their stock as he said that it would soon take off. He wasn't able to tell her why, but they were in the process of developing Viagra. She's been berating herself ever since for not listening to that tip.

One of our tenants was a personable PR man who handled that function for the Pacific National Exhibition for two years. During that time Bernice worked with him on site for the 17 days of the exhibition. It was an interesting project, however shortly after the second session at the PNE he moved out, leaving a huge unpaid bill. Thank goodness there weren't too many tenants like that

DON THOMAS WITH GUEST AT CHRISTMAS

One of our most prolific off-site clients was Don Thomas, an architectural specification writer who worked out of his home in West Vancouver. Don was a great traveler and each Christmas would send us a long letter about his travels for that year. From 1985 to 1988 he worked in Kuwait and we received some interesting letters while he was there, telling us about the social mores and his travels to nearby countries.

Ocean Towers is a luxury co-op residence facing the ocean in the west end. They are very likely the longest continuous client for the company as they recently celebrated their 48th annual meeting. We take minutes at their AGM and throughout the year look after their accounting needs. Over the years they have had highly competent people on their board and in some cases are able to handle many details themselves.

Thomas R. Butler was a PR-man extraordinaire in the words of Joy Metcalfe. His genius created the annual Belly Flop competition at a hotel on the north shore. When the Pan Pacific Hotel opened in 1986 he had the Vancouver Fireman's band play the song, "Daisy, Daisy", while Mayor Michael Harcourt rode into the hotel on an ancient bicycle built for two with the great-great-grandaughter of Vancouver's first Mayor, Jennifer Dickson. It was Jennifer's 14th birthday and both she and Michael were dressed in old-fashioned outfits of the previous century, complete with straw boaters.

One of Tom Butler's biggest campaigns was for Pavarotti's first visit to Vancouver in 1986 (this was after I retired). Tri-C was provided with several thousand post cards, which had to be hand addressed to people all over the pacific north-west, and with a short message asking them to come and see him in Vancouver. Everyone we knew was working on these post cards. Bernice even sent some to her son Dale, in Terrace, as his waitresses had time on their hands and enjoyed doing the job. Tom Butler eventually moved to PEI and we haven't heard from him since.

Of particular interest were people in sports such as Darryl Bowie (a friend of Greg Athans), who was ranked number two Freestyle Skier in the World in 1978. He, along with his brother and sister, rented office space for a short time in 1979 and he invited us to a showing of a movie in which he was featured named "Different Slopes" – a real adventure story. Paul Winterton, who founded and ran Windsure Windsurfing, was a client for many years. It was fun to watch as he and his wife built their business and eventually sold it.

Ray Saunders is well-known in Vancouver as the man who designed the Gastown Steam Clock, one of the downtown landmarks that attract a constant stream of tourists taking pictures. Ray is one of those creative people who are happy to work on their own and he needed secretarial services from time to time.

CORNELIA OBERLANDER AND DENIZE AT GISELA'S GOOD-BYE PARTY

Cornelia Hahn Oberlander is an admirable woman for whom we did specifications. She was the landscape architect who did the work for Robson Square when it was built and shared a secret with us; the mound there contained a growing medium rather than earth. She also designed the grounds at the Museum of Anthropology and the National Gallery of Canada. She studied under Walter Gropius at Harvard and was one of the first women to graduate from Harvard in her field. She has been honoured both nationally and internationally for her work.

IATSI, the union for those who worked in film and on stage in Vancouver was a client and through their office we were often offered free or heavily discounted tickets to film or stage productions. Their members brought us a lot of work as each time they finished a movie they needed to have their resumes updated. These people were set designers, make-up artists and so on and their resumes offered a nice respite from doing architectural specifications.

And who can forget David Fairleigh, the man who owned the Hollywood Theatre? He came in regularly to have us do mailings to theatres across Canada. He bought seats from theatres that were closing or remodeling and re-sold them. Each time he came in he made sure that we had a supply of free passes to his theatre and what a bonus that was! The Hollywood is on West Broadway and is a second run theatre that runs double bills of excellent movies. It was established in 1935 by the Fairleigh family.

We attracted entrepreneurs and another interesting person was Marg Young, an eccentric woman who was a lawyer. Marg loved to collect paintings and returned from a convention in Switzerland with several pieces of very good art, which she invited us to see one evening. We were invited for dinner and found that she shared her apartment overlooking English Bay with a number of birds, who flew hither and yon with no restraints. Marg had a heart of gold and when she was handling a divorce for another client asked Bernice whether she would like to get hers at the same time – and charged not a penny!

BOB WALDRON AND MARLIES AT HER 20 YEAR PARTY

Bob Waldron had an interesting business, yet it was full of tragedy. He and his two employees worked full time investigating airplane part failures and crashes as well as helicopter crashes. Once in a while we had a tape to transcribe which he had dictated in a helicopter (not an easy task). He was famous for bringing in a case of wine as a Christmas gift every year.

Craig Aspinall had an office next door on Homer Street and he did a lot of public relations for the Social Credit political party. When they were in power Craig always went to the Vancouver Cabinet Office in Robson Square when the cabinet was meeting there. Things were very busy when the Cabinet was in session and he soon asked Bernice to accompany him. She found it interesting to see how the media waited just outside the door to interview any Ministers or the Premier as they left the office. Craig's other claim to fame is his annual Christmas Eve open house and his annual summer barbeque, hosted by he and his wife Ginny.

My years with Tri-C were very rewarding and I always felt that I gained more than I was ever able to give back from the many, many wonderful people I met and worked with over the years. I owe so much to so many people for their support and encouragement along the way, including my family. I can never thank each one who worked with me during the years 1957 to 1984, nor each valued client who came through our various doors in those years. Each job we received, no matter how small it may have seemed at the time, added another building block or a little cement to keep the whole structure growing, until today, in the year 2007, the company known as Support Services Unlimited is still operating on a much larger and different concept than I could ever have dreamed of back in 1957.

Thank you and God bless you all as you
continue your journey through life.

Chapter Five
BERNICE - CHANGING DIRECTION

Surprises

O nce Denize had retired in October of 1984 I was able to move to her desk and finally sit in the chair I had pictured myself in four years previously. It was however, quite a shock to find out how demanding the SME members were. For some time now Denize had been able to devote most of her time to them, and I quickly realized that I couldn't handle three associations (SME, Canadian Club and WBA) and still run the business. In my plans to become sole owner I knew there would be no time for courses, and decided to leave Toastmistress, leaving me free to do the work, not to learn how any longer. That freed up some evening time but I still couldn't stretch myself enough to do two people's work.

I had hired Sherry as receptionist/telephone answering, however she wasn't yet able to produce very much in the way of typing. Marlies had moved into my slot; and was doing a good job of meeting clients and handling a heavy load of typing but I didn't yet want to add association management to her work load.

In January 1985 I spoke with Annette, my youngest daughter, who had worked with us briefly when she graduated from high school. She was working in collections for Visa and was most unhappy as she wanted to be in marketing. I asked if she'd like to come back to Tri-C and she said "Yes". Her typing speed was low and needed improvement, however she was good on the telephone and she took on responsibility for WBA and eventually learned to take minutes at their board meetings and organize dinners.

As time went on I found that she was very good at office rentals, even renting the small office at the back which was next door to the men's washroom. She also took over collection calls, something I didn't really enjoy doing, and she considered a piece of cake. Annette stayed with us until she and her husband John Fakaro moved to Kelowna in 1989 and I was always grateful for her support and her natural marketing ability.

People Problems

Before long there was insurrection in the ranks as I received a call from Denize telling me that some of the staff members were unhappy and asking her to intercede. Of course she wouldn't tell me who had called and we agreed on the phone that I would handle it. I called a quick staff meeting the next morning to ask that anyone who was unhappy to come to me. No one ever did, however as I look back I can see that I was defensive and probably didn't present the opportunity to talk to me in a manner that was inviting to those who were unhappy. I did determine that it would have been better to release all employees when Denize left and rehire them on my terms. Sometimes the right answer becomes very clear after the fact. Oh, that we could see it ahead of time!

Later in 1985 I hired Nora Goldberg to work with us on team building projects as I knew that to be productive my employees had to be happy in their work. We were now six people and I had much to learn about managing them. My big concern when I took over the company was how to manage paying everyone on the last day of the month and then the next day paying the rent. It was several months before I was comfortable enough not to worry any longer about the cash flow. Now I learned how to get a dialogue going with my people so that their concerns were addressed. I soon learned that everyone needed to be involved in upcoming changes. I remember very well a quote which said that people will support that which they helped to create, and it became part of my management philosophy.

A maintenance job that required regular attention was for our two photocopiers, two so that if one was down the other could handle the load. Pitney Bowes provided regular maintenance as part of our contract;

however we were very fussy about quality and called them often to come in. We saw these fellows so often that they were always invited to our Christmas parties. My son Lance was no longer servicing our copier as he had moved to head office in Toronto.

CHRISTMAS PARTY 1986, L-R FRONT, ANNETTE DECAIRE, BERNICE DAVIDSON, LORNA EGAN, REAR, GISELA BREIG, MARLIES MCGUIRE, ALICIA PHILLIPS, DENIZE CALLAWAY, IRENE EGGER AND LOUISE DADEY. GISELA, DENIZE AND IRENE CAME BACK FOR THE PARTY.
PHOTO COURTESY OF ROBERT BLAKE

Upgrading Equipment

As personnel problems leveled out I knew that the next hurdle to be overcome was to move our word processing to an IBM system. We already had an IBM computer to do bookkeeping, which Irene handled, and it was now time to replace the almost eight year old Xerox dedicated word processor. The easy part was acquiring new computers; the more difficult part was transferring all the information to the new system. Two major programs were in use and Gisela recommended that we move to Microsoft Word (rather than Word Perfect, which was in broader use). In the long run this was a very wise decision, based mainly on capability to do architectural specifications, which were a major portion of the words we processed. We had a lot of material stored on the early eight-inch disks and brought in a young man who worked full time for several weeks to transfer everything.

Even though we had been doing accounting on an IBM PC our program was already outdated so I bought a copy of ACCPAC General Ledger and proceeded to install it myself. This turned out to be a frustrating exercise as my experience with computers was minimal and my accounting expertise was relatively new. Many times I phoned Lance in Toronto to help me out of a tight spot. I spent many evenings and week-ends setting this up and did a lot of hand wringing in the process.

Goodbye to Good Employees

Gisela was preparing to leave in March 1986 after 23 years with Tri-C, as she now realized that she needed a job which would provide some pension during retirement. She had been accepted at UBC Engineering and knew that she had enough years yet to work that would provide a comfortable pension later on. It was difficult to see Gisela leave because she was extremely capable and dependable, but as she looked to her future she needed something I couldn't give her, so we had a big party for her and wished her well on her way.

I would have liked to move Marlies into the word processing position, however she preferred more customer contact, and word processing was primarily a task which required more focus on the work, rather than on the client. In fact, for quite some time Marlies resisted learning the word processor. However, when she did finally decide that she was ready, she learned it in no time and really enjoyed her newfound skill.

The next person to leave was Irene who had married Ralph Egger a few years before and now planned to move to Alberta. Irene was an excellent bookkeeper and was the person who had told me earlier that I really needed to learn the accounting process, for which I have been eternally grateful. She later established her own secretarial service in Lethbridge.

Finding good replacements for such capable women was not easy. I made a few bad decisions, however was able to suggest to people who were not able to work in our fast-paced environment that they look elsewhere for work. This was so much better than firing people outright and it also let them keep their dignity.

1986 Was a Big Year

At last all of the loans to buy the business were paid off and I was ready to give a new look to our premises. Shelly Mirich was a client and also an award-winning designer and I always believed in using our clients wherever possible. It made good sense to keep them in business. Shelly created some interior designs for us that were truly original. He did a mural for the entrance with a faux desk and filing cabinet. Doesn't the picture look like a real desk and filing cabinet?

NEW ENTRANCE AT 1250 HOMER

Inside we had room dividers that looked like huge rolls of computer paper (in those days printers used a continuous roll of paper). The part I really loved was the new carpet with a ying~yang design.

RE-DESIGNED RECEPTION AREA 1250 HOMER

For two years I had been doing volunteer work with the YMCA, which was located half a block from my first apartment. I had learned to respect the work that the Y did in the city and was pleased to be invited in 1986 to sit on their board, and a year later on the executive. Now I was in a position to see how a non-profit made use of the volunteer talent available and how board members were trained. This gave me insight into how my non-profit groups could improve board relations. As I volunteered my time to work for the Y I was rewarded with trips to such places as Quebec City and Seoul, Korea. This was surely a mutually beneficial arrangement.

It was early 1986 and Expo was coming to Vancouver. Business was booming and we were bursting at the seams. My aim now became to fine tune the business so that it became a model to replicate. Somehow I was never satisfied enough with the fine tuning to get to the second part. Perhaps the fates could see the far reaches of my abilities, or, to put it another way, perhaps my subconscious knew my capabilities.

Tough Jobs

Meanwhile, along the way there were lots of challenges. Expo 86 lasted from May to October and the West Gate was a short walk from our office. Our landlord leased out the parking lot at night and on week-ends for the duration of Expo and provided us with four passes that our tenants could use if they were working outside office hours or wanted to visit Expo. Somehow free parking for Expo wasn't seen as a big benefit compared to the loss of 24 hour parking to which everyone was accustomed. There was a big hullabaloo and the tenants had a meeting and offered to negotiate with my landlord. I refused to let them intercede or accompany me to "get a better deal". It was the male tenants who were complaining and I had other concerns to handle.

I knew that for the six months of Expo, street parking would be at a premium and we needed to free up some parking spaces for our off-premises clients. I searched for some off-site parking for myself and two employees who used their cars. The best "deal" I could find cost three times the usual rate and had to be paid in cash. Our parking lot was clearly signed for private parking but several times a day we had to call the tow truck because people disregarded the signs. It was a great advantage however to be able to visit Expo and not pay for parking. It was a wonderful showcase to the world and a once-in-a-lifetime experience. It was also a great year to host the International convention for Sales & Marketing Executives International. In 1985 I'd attended their convention in Dallas, Texas as preparation for hosting this year.

One day I noticed a client standing over Marlies as she worked and that was something we discouraged, so I knew that she hadn't invited the looking-over-the-shoulder that was going on. When he left she said that she was under the gun to get his job done as it had to be completed the next day. I knew that this client was famous for paying late; often payment for one job didn't come in until another was needed. I mulled over the situation that night and decided that it couldn't continue. I called him first thing the next morning and said that it had become necessary to put him on a cash basis because we couldn't afford to carry him for long periods of time without payment. I further told him that we were looking at instituting a rush charge for jobs that were needed in a hurry but wouldn't add that on to the current bill.

I knew that we might lose a client over this but my reasoning was that this client was not the type of person we needed. Sure enough he went to someone else for his next job but was back to see us within a few months. And he paid in full when his job was finished.

Don Cameron, the accountant, had told me when I became a partner that for the first few years I would likely do many tasks myself that in later years I'd hire others to do. I wasn't about to tackle regular janitorial duties, however decided that I could replace the long fluorescent bulbs that were everywhere. I had to go to Chinatown to buy them on a Saturday morning and would bring back a six month supply and store them in the "safe". The other task was cleaning venetian blinds, a job I frankly hated. I would take one down and spread it out on the carpet, clean it, dry it and put it up again. It took a month of Saturdays every year to do this job. After a few years I found a company that would come in, take them all away and bring them back clean the following day, then re-hang them in the offices. It was a happy day when I hired them for the first time!

The Payoffs

Now it seemed that all my years of frugality were paying off. I had walked to work for eight years, not only to free up money to invest in the business but also so that I could afford to visit my parents in Toronto a couple of times each year. When Lance visited to see Expo he helped me pick out a car, my beloved blue Toyota Celica which was brand new. That summer I also bought new furniture; a sofa bed, two custom upholstered chairs and a teak dining table and chairs. I quit smoking for the first time, and then in November made my first trip to Hawaii. My daughter Annette was marrying John Fakaro on the beach at Waikiki. When I saw the videos of the wedding it was quite apparent how chubby I'd become since I'd quit smoking and was no longer walking to work. Sooner or later I'd have to do something about that.

GISELA AND MARLIES AT THE PICNIC IN STANLEY PARK

National Association of Secretarial Services

In my search for expertise I had found this group, which was headquartered in Florida. They produced a monthly newsletter and provided opportunities for training at an annual convention. One of the key benefits was a set of "Industry Standards", which were particularly valuable as I trained new staff members. The standards set out the time required to produce a certain amount of work, without specifying how much to charge. We set our hourly charges by comparing our rates to those charged by other local companies.

In 1987 I booked to attend the June convention in St. Petersburg, Florida. I'd never been to Florida so this would be another new experience for me. Soon I would have the third computer program we needed to give us all round expertise. It was a wonderful experience to attend the workshops and meet other business owners from all over the United States. The most valuable thing I brought back was knowledge of a new invoicing program written for secretarial services. At last I would be able to get rid of the cumbersome manual process we used to produce invoices every month. There were so many details to be compiled and I had been searching everywhere for a program that would bill both time and other services. I could hardly believe that someone had created a program just for us, and once it was installed our invoices went out on the first day of each month. That conference was a wonderful way to incorporate business and pleasure.

For a couple of years we hosted a picnic at Stanley Park in the summer and that was a lot of fun. There were contests for the best hat or t-shirt, fish pond for the little children, watermelon eating contests for the older children, egg toss, three-legged race, sack race and the contests ended with everyone participating in a tug-of-war. I think everyone enjoyed playing like a kid again, leaving behind the formality of the office. We didn't continue them after Annette left because I found it too stressful, wondering if the weather was going to be good to us.

Financial Planning

Certainly one of the best moves I made during my business life was to use the services of a financial planner. One of my tenants, Peggy Inverarity, recommended a man named Lawrence Winters at Vancouver Financial Planning because he had given her some good advice. Even though the Association of Financial Planners had been a client for a number of years I hadn't availed myself of their services. Now I was at a stage where I had paid off the debts in the business and needed to decide how much I could take out each year for personal use and investment.

I found Lawrie approachable and helpful and he suggested to me that he could help me both in keeping my business profitable and in planning my personal financial future. I soon realized that self-employed people are at a distinct advantage in this regard because they have the ability to regulate their personal cash flow for tax purposes, and little did I realize in the beginning how important that would become. He soon had me bringing in the corporate financial statements and creating a personal financial statement. Added to this was a document which set out my dreams. Now, I never did get the Jaguar convertible but Laurie later helped me put things in context and I was able to realize that a Jaguar really wasn't necessary for happiness in life.

We set up a system whereby I took my company financial statements to Lawrie every six months and he evaluated them and gave me his feedback.

Sometimes it would be, "Your salary expense is too high for your revenue. What can you do about that?" Never did Laurie visit the office and this kept his fees low enough that I could afford them. Also he billed the company, not me personally for his services.

One day Lawrie explained to me that something I really needed was to own an apartment or house so that when I retired my living expenses would be relatively low. By now I was in my early 50's but not looking at retiring for a long time yet, however the thought of owning an apartment was appealing and soon I found one at 16th Avenue and Granville. The neighbourhood was interesting with lots of art galleries and restaurants within a few blocks and I could look out my window as I ate breakfast and watch the cruise ships coming into harbour during the summer months.

Within two years I sold the apartment and bought a house just below Grouse Mountain in North Vancouver. The house was a bit of a stretch for me but Lawrie showed me how to manage and one of his hints was to go to Vancity Credit Union where I could get a mortgage with a lower down payment than the bank would offer. Also I bought a house with a 2 bedroom ground floor apartment, in which I lived, and rented the top floor to tenants. The house became an excellent investment for me as a self-employed person has no company pension for their later years, and when I sold it six years later it brought a good return of tax free money.

I had neither the expertise nor the time for investing and Lawrie looked after that for me. Finally when I sold the business I had to begin paying personally for his services; however it was money well spent. And over the years the benefits that accrued were significant. I believe the biggest benefit was not in tracking what had transpired over the past year but in planning for a future which was still many years ahead. To quote the Mastercard advertising, financial planning is one of those services that is "priceless".

Staffing

My experience in personnel with national companies gave me some confidence, but very little of the skill I needed to hire competent staff. Over time I had the best success with hiring young people as they graduated from school. But first I had to make some mistakes. Thank goodness there was such a thing as a probationary period. Along the way I hired a young person who couldn't spell and someone suggested later that they believed she was on drugs. After coaching her for a time I did encourage her to look elsewhere as we really needed good spelling in the days before spell-check. Then there was the woman who refused to file or clean her fingernails. This was someone whose job included registration at downtown hotels for events. Ever after I checked out fingernails when I was interviewing.

Happier times came when I found exceptional people who were skilled, had common sense and a good work ethic.

OLGA FERREIRA

Olga Ferreira came to us just as she finished a two year accounting course at BCIT. She had grown up in the Okanagan where her parents had an orchard and her father had her doing his bookkeeping so that she would have some experience when she graduated. Olga had such a happy manner and was willing to tackle any job. She was a good team player and was able to focus on the job at hand.

TEENA AT ONE OF OUR PARTIES WITH GUESTS FROM THE WBA

Teena Keizer came to us after finishing a secretarial course. Teena had some previous experience in retail and over time I've found that those with retail experience are easier to train in customer service. Teena often alerted me to clients who needed more extensive service.

JIM BLATHERWICK

Jim Blatherwick was a new graduate with a degree in geography who found it difficult to find a job in that field. He had great enthusiasm for his work and always looked at the big picture. For a young man who had grown up in a privileged family he had a great deal of common sense.

MARLIES ARRIVING IN A LIMO, 1991

Most importantly, Marlies McGuire was a dependable, long time employee who was wonderfully loyal over the years. In fact, she holds the record for the longest tenure of any employee – 27 years. She was happy to take over most of the work for the Canadian Club in later years and did a wonderful job for them. We had a big party for her 20th anniversary in 1991 and she came to work in a limo.

She actually worked all day and then in the evening we had a reception with food and drinks and a big anniversary cake.

MARLIES IN THE OFFICE WITH HER WELCOME SIGN

Critical Decision

It was January of 1991 when I drove to the office on a cold, rainy Sunday morning. There was always a pile of catch-up work to be done and Sunday was a good day to work undisturbed. As I pulled into the parking lot at 1250 Homer I saw a big sign, "For Sale". At first I felt disbelief, then anger. How could the building owner do such a thing without notifying me? After all, I was the prime tenant, renting the entire first floor and warehouse space upstairs!

Once inside I called the owner at home to verify that what I'd seen was true – and yes, it was. And I was truly dumbfounded. How could I possibly rent furnished offices with a "for sale" sign out front? I knew that there were decisions to be made and quickly.

Wanting to put some physical distance between the problem and myself, I picked up a lined pad, stopped to buy a package of cigarettes (my off/on crutch and comfort) and headed for home. And there in my fifth floor apartment overlooking the city and ocean I sat down to plan my future. I knew there were three options:

1. Stay and hope the new owner didn't want the ground floor
2. Take staff and clients to another location
3. Change the focus of the business

My lease ran out at the end of March, leaving me free to pursue any of the options. I quickly discarded the first, as I wanted to make the decisions for my company, not depend on someone else's agenda. The second was very appealing because I knew that I had the expertise to be welcomed in a number of locations.

Within a short time I had considered the pros and cons of each and decided on the last option. Many of our tenants were sales offices of national companies and there was a trend to set up BC salesmen with computers and faxes at home, rather than renting sales offices. Also, there was a growing segment of the business wherein we supplied a virtual office to small non-profit associations and also provided them with administrative services. With these clients we had more ability to schedule their work as we were in charge of initiating most tasks.

I knew too that there were many packaged offices in Vancouver but few association management companies, and I enjoyed being unique. This was the era when executives in most large companies were first provided with computers, leaving them with less need for support staff as everyone was learning to type. Hindsight tells me that this same phenomenon left them with fewer resources to provide to their favourite non-profit, leaving the non-profits with a greater need for association management services.

Closing down a successful business sector is not an easy decision. It had taken the hard work of many people to create such an enterprise, but primarily the vision of one woman who led them. I was not that woman, but I had bought the business from her, and now was about to change it substantially.

Once the decision was made there were three things to be accomplished almost simultaneously: notify the staff, notify the tenants and find new premises. Until the last item was complete I wasn't going to give notice to the landlord. First thing Monday morning I brought the staff together and told them that I was going to look immediately for new premises as the building was now for sale.

I asked them to not offer this information to clients, however if they were asked, to reply that I was looking for new office space.

I soon found that Yaletown provided some distinct advantages, primarily lower rentals and more accessible parking. One of the buildings I looked at on Hastings Street required a $20 deposit at the parking lot, and would give you a refund of the unused portion when you left. I knew that our clients would not appreciate such a system. Time was of the essence here as I knew that rumours would soon fly and I wanted to make an announcement as soon as possible, certainly before the end of the month. Now I focused on Yaletown and found an office just a block away. A former client, Joe Wai, had just moved out of the space and alerted me that there would soon be a construction site outside our window. This gave me the information I needed to negotiate a good deal. Joe also told me that the landlord was fair and dependable and I appreciated that information.

Before month end we had a deal and I was able to notify my tenants that we would be moving to new space, but would no longer be sub-leasing packaged offices. Everyone was on a month to month basis and this gave them more than two months to find new premises, which some did, while others moved to a home office. Now, with satisfaction, I told my landlord that we were moving at the end of our lease.

Finding My Strengths

This was when I came to realize how much I enjoyed this new challenge. I had known for some time that my talents did not lie in managing. I much preferred initiating new ideas, which is why I enjoyed association management. Every year there was a new board of directors; and those directors soon came to rely on my advice.

The biggest challenge would be to move into space which was one-fifth the size of our present quarters. Seven times I did the floor plan before it was finalized, and when it was done I knew exactly what we could take and what had to be sold or otherwise disposed of. The only new item we needed was a reception desk as ours was very large and impossible to move. In most cases I kept the best furniture and sold the rest. I was able to co-ordinate the filing cabinets and after the move they were all black. The cabinets that needed to be painted were sent out the week before the move and delivered to us after the move was completed. At the same time our little bar fridge was painted black and delivered with them.

One of the most expensive parts of the move was the telephone system; however sales of excess furniture more than covered all our moving costs. I arranged to have an auction house pick up everything that remained unsold.

We were lucky that Easter week-end came at the end of March that year and the movers came in Thursday evening at 5:00 pm. Late that night everything was delivered to the new location, however one of the men told me that he had doubted that everything was going to fit – and he didn't know that several items would be delivered on Monday!

Marlies was good enough to come in on Good Friday and work with me to bring some sort of order out of chaos. Then on Saturday I went back to 1250 Homer to pick up some odds and ends. We continued to go back to pick up mail for several months as the post office wouldn't forward the multiple addressed mail that we received.

In those days we didn't close on Easter Monday, however this year we told the clients that we would be closed. This gave each staff member time to put their own desk in order, time for the telephone system to be moved, time to have all the computers and printer set up, and time for the newly painted filing cabinets and refrigerator to be delivered. It seemed like some sort of minor miracle when we opened for business on Tuesday April 2nd as an association management company.

There are times when I wonder where my energy came from in those days. During that month I sold my apartment and bought a house which I moved into on May 23rd. Then in August I took a two week trip to Taipai, Hong Kong and Seoul, where I represented the YMCA at an international conference.

Changing the Name

Reality set in very quickly. When we did the invoicing at the end of April I was amazed at the low numbers, yet I shouldn't have been, and of course our expenses were now less than they had been at the other location. I could very quickly see that an aggressive marketing campaign was necessary. The first step was a letter to the directors of each of the associations we managed. This announced our move and invited them to think about our capabilities for any other group they worked with. It is a common thing for directors to be on more than one board and this is how most of our new business came in.

I learn many things from books and one that I read now had a huge impact. It was by Michael Gerber and was called "The E-Myth: Why Most Small Businesses Don't Work and What to Do About It". Soon I began working with Michael Gerber's staff, learning how to grow my business. And it was from this work that our new name came into being and was announced near the end of 1992. We were now doing business as "Support Services Unlimited" to reflect the new range of services which were more management, rather than administrative.

In 1993 I brought Michael Gerber to town to speak to our home based clients. I had read Michael's books, and admired his ideas, then in 1992 had become a client. His concept was amazing. He provided coaching services by telephone. I never did meet my coach in person, and in fact worked with more than one coach. The first woman I spoke with worked from her home in Saskatchewan, and then later I worked with a man from California. This was my first experience with coaching and I thoroughly enjoyed this method of learning. I was able to analyze my business as never before and accomplish changes.

This was where I began to set up formal procedures and document them in a comprehensive procedure manual. July – August were the slow months of the year and this was when we did some work on the manual. The basic concept was to document every job so that anyone could come in and do the work. This was most helpful with a new hire. Also I learned that no job ever stayed the same. Each new person brought something of themselves, and all we had to do was document the changes to stay current. Many years later, when it came time to sell the business, the manual helped greatly in the selling process.

Hosting Michael Gerber was quite an experience. I was used to hiring venues and dealing with speakers, however none had been quite as specific as Michael. He specified that the only items on stage were to be a small table containing a water pitcher and glass and a bud base with one red rose. Beside the table he specified a stool of a certain height plus a portable microphone. He provided the script for his introduction. He was a popular speaker, however as a client I didn't need to pay him; neither did I have to provide his accommodation, so this was a great deal for me. In return I provided him with an audience of entrepreneurs who had just received a free breakfast. Now they were hungry for the kind of inspiration and information he was so good at giving.

There were a few lean months before the marketing program began to pay off, however I believe that completing the move without incurring any out-of-pocket expense was the key to remaining afloat until revenue increased. At the same time I did not make any unnecessary purchases until our sales increased. And slowly and surely sales did increase; not only from new clients but by providing extra services for existing clients. Conferences are a great source of revenue, particularly when they are international in scale. In those days it meant huge mailings, follow-up emails, and generally increased revenue for almost a year.

More Learning Experiences

Then, just as I thought we were over the hump, one of my employees took CIPS, our biggest client, away. I was devastated by this, as I had been particularly flexible with this employee. She was still attending university and I kept her on full time over the summer when she was out of school (and our business was slow). After this there was a clause in every contract to protect us against that ever happening again. I soon realized what a blow it is to lose both your largest client and a very bright employee.

In 1992 one of our clients approached me to see whether I would be interested in taking my expertise to other countries. This man was the treasurer of one of our associations and I had known him for some years so I listened carefully to what he proposed. He had contacts in Asian countries where people wanted to set themselves up in business but lacked the knowledge of what was needed to begin. He proposed that I journey to one of these countries for a one month period and assist a company in their start-up phase. Primarily I would provide a list of physical items needed to set up an operation such as mine, plus provide an operations manual and initial training. I had been in Asia the year before and in each country had visited a business similar to mine, so I had some background for such a project.

I was intrigued by this offer and we began negotiations. In my excitement I spoke with my good friend Ed Chan, a landed immigrant from Malaysia and his advice to me was to be very careful. He insisted that I be provided with a room in a five star hotel as anything less would not be satisfactory. I also mentioned this opportunity to Rod McCloy, who was then President of the Canadian Club of Vancouver. Rod is a lawyer and he very kindly offered to vet any proposal that was provided to me. When the offer came I forwarded it to Rod and he added just two items. Neither of the items he added was accepted and with that I backed away. The project really appealed to me, but I wasn't about to be someone's slave. I have always been thankful for the assistance that Rod offered, especially as it was free of charge.

In 1993 I became President of Canadian Office Services Association, whose members ran either secretarial services or packaged offices. This gave me the opportunity to see how an association runs from the inside out. I had background in Toastmistress, as both a member and President, and also as a board member with the YMCA, however this was different. COSA was a stand-alone group, not part of a larger association. The President was really the engine that drove the group and I was determined to provide some structure, based on my experience with many associations of varying sizes. We had a planning session at the beginning of the year and I was able to delegate most jobs to members of the board. We set up a schedule of board meetings and I set up an award to be presented at each meeting called the "Panache Award". It gave me great pleasure to present a rose as a symbol of the award to each recipient. In each issue of the newsletter I described why someone had been given this award, which highlighted creative ideas. The first rose went to Hardy Bunn whose business card showed her title as *Supreme Commander*, rather than the usual president or owner.

That year COSA held a full day marketing workshop, held our first Christmas party and gained some exposure for our group by volunteering at an annual telethon. We worked on teaching members about the concept of a procedures manual and I believe that we had more members during that year than at any other time. At year end I invited the board members to my house where I treated them to a thank you lunch. Much of what I accomplished was learned from watching successful leaders of the associations we managed.

COSA BOARD MEMBERS, JUNE 1994: L-R, SHERYL SMALE, DEBBIE MOCHINSKI, GWEN TURPIN, CARREL ALDEN, KARLINE MARK ENG, BERNICE

I believe that it is important to create learning experiences for ourselves as time goes on. Sometimes we begin to feel that we have everything in hand and enjoy the feeling of competency but this can be fatal. The world doesn't stay the same and neither should our companies. The owner of a small business has more freedom than anyone working in a large corporation. If you see something that needs to be changed you simply change it. And decisions can be made and implemented quickly. I always liked to "stir the pot" regularly and never let my employees become too comfortable in their work. We all needed challenges on a regular basis.

Creating an Exit Strategy

Late in 1996 I was approached by a woman named Dawn Thier, from the U.S., who wanted to become a partner. She had seen our website and found the business interesting. The idea was intriguing to me and I was open to such a proposal. Thus we began an email correspondence and she indicated that she would be visiting Vancouver in a few months, when we could meet.

I spoke about this possibility to my financial planner, Lawrie Winters, and he advised me to get some indication from her regarding her financial resources. After some time I learned that she was prepared to invest $5,000 to become a partner and I quickly let her know that she wasn't in the ballpark with that amount of money.

This offer opened up a new scenario for me and I began to wonder if I should look locally for a partner as I was now 62. I spoke with my accountant, (now my daughter-in-law Nancy) who reminded me that the four year partnership with Denize had seemed long to me, and her advice was to look for a buyer rather than a partner.

For some time I had been looking at each of my employees to see whether one of them might have the entrepreneurial spirit but none had that interest, even though they were very capable workers. I have two daughters who would be competent to take over such an enterprise but neither was interested. Annette had worked with us for several years while Rhonda had filled in once for a few weeks, and they both knew what was required. I was in no rush to sell and decided that there were some things I needed to do before I put it on the market:

- Continue to build sales
- Update the physical premises
- Finish the procedure manual.

At the same time there were things I would not do, primarily not incur any long range commitments in the way of leases. We were now in the second year of the office lease and I had one 10 year lease on telephones and I believed it best to keep leases at that level. I no longer leased my car through the company, just charged the company for the use of the car each month.

First on the list was building sales. The Association of Professional Economists was planning an international conference in Vancouver for November of 1997 and I persuaded them that we could handle all of the conference details and it was not necessary for them to hire a conference co-coordinator. This turned out to be an interesting venture with the two Conference Co-chairs named John De Wolf (the local president) and Leo De Beaver, who was with the Ontario Pension Plan. You couldn't possibly dream up a pair of names like that! It also turned out to be a great revenue generator. The promotion pieces went all over the world and we sent out many emails. That conference stretched our resources but it really increased the revenue stream.

Next on the list was upgrading the visual look of the office. Everything was blah! White walls, blue dividers and grey carpet left us with lots of room to add some zing. I found a decorator who asked me for my favourite colour, which was hot pink. We ended up with a dark version of hot pink on one wall, along with some wonderful artwork from my favourite gallery. Then we found an interesting fabric and had all the chairs covered in that same fabric; steno chairs as well as client arm chairs in the reception area. This new look gave everyone a lift.

Last on the list, and most difficult, was completing the procedure manual. This type of thing is not my forte, and we had been working at it now for several years yet never finishing. When July came I was determined that we would complete it by the end of the summer. We had instructions for opening the office, and closing it up again at night. A dress code was created and hiring procedures were put on paper at last. All the information on each client was updated and general procedures that were the same for each client, such as how to do a bank deposit, were put into writing. As an example, we never went to the bank in person to do a deposit, as it was a lower cost for the client if we sent it by courier. It was the same concept for printing; it was either sent by courier or picked up by the printer's representative. Through the years our procedures were built on the concept of 'what is the most efficient way we can do the job on behalf of the client'. This was a most valuable inheritance from Denize. The procedures themselves may change but not the underlying concepts.

That fall was very busy with the conference as well as our other clients and when December came it was time to take another look at selling the business. At this time I looked at the COSA members to see if there might be a possibility that one of them might want to buy, however there didn't seem to be a likely prospect.

Meanwhile I had been unsuccessful in bringing in a new association client. It was the first time that had happened. In the past I had always been successful when I prepared a proposal so this was a new experience. I thought about it for a while and decided that if I were in the shoes of the client, I probably wouldn't hire a woman my age to run my association for the next five years. This was the thing that verified my decision to move on. It really was time to take my leave. And now I shared my plan with the staff. Marlies was adamant that she would leave when I did and I knew it would be difficult for her to work for yet another boss. She had been there longer than I had and knew that there would be the inevitable changes when someone new came in.

Finding a Buyer

Early in February 1998 I contacted Tony Mumford, a business broker, and that was a most fortunate phone call. He did a marvelous job of bringing people in to look at the business. In fact I couldn't believe that so many people might be interested in doing this work. After a couple of months I settled on a man who had made the best offer, although I had some reservations about how I would introduce him to our clients. Tony could see that I wasn't really thrilled and he must have placed another newspaper ad because before I had time to finalize the decision he found Donna Denham and brought her to see me.

Donna had good background working with non-profit associations, and I could see that she was highly qualified. The only drawback was a lack of funds. When she was able to make an offer the initial payment was less, however there was no question about which person would be better qualified to carry on the business. Now Donna and I had an agreement and it included a full month in which we could do the hand-over. Donna came in June 1, 1998 and I made my exit on June 30th.

Never did I suspect that I would spend another seven years working in the business, either one or two days per week, however it made for a very comfortable retirement plan for me. I still was able to spend the month of August with my son in Toronto, and take a long planned two month trip to Europe the following spring. I believe that our clients benefited from the close association between Donna and me and I've been forever grateful to Tony Mumford for introducing us.

DENIZE, BERNICE, DONNA, 1998

Chapter Six
BERNICE REMEMBERS SOME ASSOCIATION CLIENTS

S ales and Marketing Executives came to us when we were on Burrard Street and the contacts were John Hill and Carson Whyte. It was the first big association we brought in. This group had an evening meeting each month from September through June, and also ran sales courses at UBC. They had a board of directors who met each month and Denize took their minutes. Soon she was booking the hotel for their meetings and ordering meals. We mailed out a meeting notice and took reservations for dinner. They had a big flat box (3 feet x 2 feet) full of name badges which had to be taken to each meeting. Their speakers at the dinner meetings were interesting and Denize stayed to collect the name badges at the end of the evening, which meant that she (and later I) was exposed to a good deal of marketing expertise.

RANDY SINGER, SME PRESIDENT 1990-91, GEORGE DEDRICK, SME PRESIDENT 1976-77
PHOTO COURTESY TOR BENGTSON

SME's courses at UBC were held in the evening and were two different types. One was a three year diploma course in Sales & Marketing Management and was taught by UBC professors. The other was a ten week course called the Vansec Sales Course, taught originally by Jim Tindle and later by Laurence Lovett. We handled the registration for both courses and the revenue provided the lifeblood for SME, and good revenue for Tri-C.

LAURENCE LOVETT RECITING HIS VERSION OF THE NIGHT BEFORE CHRISTMAS,
WITH DENIZE AND MARLIES IN THE BACKGROUND

The Reform Party of Canada started out at 1250 Homer Street with Ron Gamble. Ron ran a beverage company out of our office and out of an office in Seattle, Washington. Ron, director of the Reform Association in B.C. became a co-founder of the new federal reform party, formed in Winnipeg, Manitoba in 1987, and was elected to the party's first Executive Council.

Ron Gamble with Marlies

Ron became involved with the Reform Party of British Columbia (which predated the federal party) in 1983, which consented to the use of the federal Reform Party name. Not all of the national leaders, including Preston Manning, wanted provincial parties formed and therefore Ron had no support from the national organization. Ron, an independent thinker, went ahead anyway to focus on reform provincially.

Ron soon had a board formed of like minded people and he rented extra desk space from us for Reform BC, where both staff and volunteers did administrative work for the party. In later years, at 1007 Homer, we became the office for the party as it grew by leaps and bounds in 1995-96. Eventually Reform BC opened a large office in Surrey and that was the end of our affiliation with them.

The Western Businesswomen's Association was founded by Audrey Paterson and was a lively organization when they came to us in 1979. The members were a mix of businesswomen; some came from large corporations, while others were entrepreneurs and this made for a strong organization as each member had something to learn from the others. Here again we stayed for the monthly dinner and learned from the speakers, who were sometimes inspirational and at other times informative. This was where I learned how to publish a newsletter, as Audrey came to the office on week-ends to show me how it was done. I learned to play golf with these women and in time donated a cup for their annual tournament.

EVELYN FROESE RECEIVES TRI-C ROSE BOWL TROPHY FROM BERNICE AT COYOTE CREEK GOLF CLUB, 1991

CAFP, the Canadian Association of Financial Planners was a growing organization when they came to us. Previously they had been run by a volunteer member from his office, but as the group grew the work became more than a volunteer wanted to provide. We didn't attend the monthly meetings however we did produce a newsletter for them on a monthly basis. Their big revenue producer each year was the annual Planning School, and of course this produced good revenue for both Tri-C and SSU. In later years they merged with another group to become ADVOCIS and Donna will tell you about what has transpired there.

The Canadian Club came to our office when their full time secretary died, and they could see that their membership dues wouldn't support the office they had been renting and pay the going rate for a full time secretary. It had been a labour of love for the former secretary, who was retired and had been paid a small retainer. They arrived with furniture and typewriters and endless files. The Club was a national organization which had been set up early in the last century to fund speakers to travel across Canada to bring both cultural and political messages in person. When an election was called we would receive requests to speak from all national leaders and often organized such a luncheon in 10 days.

BERNICE GREETING PRIME MINISTER JOHN TURNER WITH JEAN CORMIER IN THE BACKGROUND, AUGUST 1984 PHOTO COURTESY JACK FLOWERDEW

In the days before television the Club was a going concern, however was on the downturn when they came to us with 1,400 members. The numbers continued to drop as fewer business men could afford to spend two hours for a downtown lunch. Today Toronto is the only club that still operates on a weekly basis and the Vancouver club hosts about six events per year. They recently celebrated their centennial and a new president is bringing new energy to the Club. With this group I had the opportunity to work with many extremely talented men and women and have been forever grateful for the experience.

An offshoot of the Canadian Club was the Jack Webster Foundation. In 1986 the club president, Jean Cormier spearheaded a dinner to honour

Jack Webster, a long time broadcaster in Vancouver. It was so successful that a board was formed to set up a foundation to honour broadcasters and print media in Jack's name on an annual basis. For at least 10 years that foundation ran out of our office, and each year the submissions would pour in at the last minute. Once the submissions were distributed to the judges our main task was to organize a gala dinner. This was always a fun event, with the opportunity to see all the media people in their finery, up close and personal. In later years the organization was taken over by a relative of one of the directors

The Canada Japan Society has been with us for more than 20 years and has been Teena's responsibility. At the first meeting she attended, she was given a draw ticket and won a trip to Hong Kong. From then on they were her darling! The purpose of the group is to form trade connections and they hold breakfasts and an annual golf tournament, along with an annual trip to a baseball game in Seattle.

In 2000 we were approached by the Kitsilano Chamber of Commerce and asked to provide administrative support for their Executive Director. They provide a good range of benefits to their members and that is something that we handle, as well as organizing events and taking minutes at their board meetings. In 2005 we were asked to organize their annual Kitsilano Soap Box Derby and Donna gave me the job. I had told her I would be leaving at the end of June, and the derby was held on June 24th, so this was my swan song, and a fun one too. I had never seen a soap box derby and soon found that it wasn't easy to find someone to bring 7,000 bales of hay into the downtown at 5 am on a Sunday morning, then come back later in the day to pick them up again. And of course there was the overall possibility of rain, which would really make a mess of things. This event brings a huge number of volunteers and about 60 young people with their motor-less cars to West Fourth Avenue on a Sunday morning. It was a real blast!

The BC Association of Kinesiologists is a group of young people, with their oldest board member just 30. There is one director who is 22, the same age as Donna's daughter Devon. They have energy galore and tons of exciting ideas. There is never a dull moment with that group.

One of the must unusual groups I worked with was the Association of International Marathons. One year they held their annual meeting here, in the week preceding the Vancouver Marathon. I took minutes for three days, and each time someone spoke there were two other voices translating, which was somewhat distracting to say the least. Once the minutes were on paper I was able to fax them to the president in Australia. This was the first year we had a fax. Can you imagine how long it would have taken to finalize the minutes if we had to depend on the mail?

I must say that one of the best clients we have, and will ever have is MMCD, the Master Municipal Contract Document Association. This is a group of municipal engineers who have compiled a master specification for municipal work in British Columbia. When they first approached us this was a completely new concept so we've been with them since the beginning. The work can be a bit technical at times, but they explain everything clearly, are patient, and consider no question we ask as unimportant or irrelevant. Several of the directors have stayed on the board since its inception, so we've known them for many years. They are very dedicated and passionate about the association and do excellent work. Their requirements are slightly different from the other clients as we sell their books and organize the courses they offer.

I wish there was room to describe all of the associations, however I've tried to show the variety of groups we serve, and illustrate how interesting it is to work with people who come from diverse backgrounds. As we learn what they are about it is almost like having the opportunity to attend a mini-university.

Chapter Seven
DONNA IS THE THIRD GENERATION

Looking for Plan B

*I*t was early 1998 and I really enjoyed working with a Notary Public and had started a small secretarial business, operating out of her office. I had purchased my own computer and laser printer which were used for both her work and my own.

My big breakthrough into the world of associations came when I landed CARP (Canadian Association of Rehabilitation Professionals) as a regular client. I did preparation for their AGM, bookkeeping, correspondence with members, and typed and compiled their newsletter, "The Rehab Review". As time went on, I soon had two more small associations as regular clients, and began to see the commonality of their needs. The Notary was considering retirement options, which meant that I needed a plan B. I thought, hmmm, I could actually specialize in associations on a regular basis, and operate a lucrative business. If I had about ten small associations we could share an office, computer equipment, phones, photocopier, etc. Thinking I was certainly the only one with this "brilliant idea" and doing this type of association work in the city, it was sure to take off.

I used to look in the classifieds regularly, and one day saw an association management business for sale, and thought, "What the heck, somebody else is doing this too. I must go and see it immediately." I called the agent and soon came in and saw Support Services and just fell in love with it. It was exactly what I had pictured – exactly! Then there was that small internal question saying, "Maybe I'm not as smart as I think I am – what if I can't actually run this business?" Initially, I didn't consider the biggest obstacle, which was money to purchase the business. I didn't think about the money or the risk at all.

A week later I came in to look at the operation more closely, spent a day reading through the SSU procedure manual (which was fabulous), and talked to Bernice about the business. I felt confident that I could manage much of it, and would have to learn the rest rather quickly. Little did I know then that it wouldn't be quite as straightforward as I anticipated - not even close. I must have been so naive in those days.

I knew that I had to have this business - it was perfect for me. It was meant to be. However, it was a lot of money to buy, and I didn't have any money – zero! Bernice offered to allow me to pay monthly payments toward the largest portion of the purchase, but I still had to come up with $20,000.

The next day or two, I can't remember the exact timing, I had a lunch appointment with my good friend Hope, who had moved to the Sunshine Coast a few years earlier. I've known Hope since I was 13, when I used to baby sit her son. Her son is about five years older than Lee-Ann, my oldest daughter. We've always stayed in touch and Hope has been a great friend and life mentor for me through the years. Her name "Hope" really symbolizes her. I live in North Vancouver, and we meet occasionally for lunch at Horseshoe Bay. As we sat there I told her about the business, and how much I loved it, and that I was trying to figure out how I could come up with the money. She said, "That sounds great, I think you should have it." I said, "I think I should have it too!", and we went on to talk about other things.

Not at all expecting what was to follow…shortly after I got home that evening Hope called to say, "I talked to Neil (her husband) and we're lending you the money." I said, "Oh no, I can't take money from you – I'll find a way". She replied, "We've decided, you're having it. Phone up those people and tell them you're buying the business. We're lending you the money and that's all there is to it. We're not the least bit concerned, and we know you will make a big success of this venture." They didn't want to look at financials or anything, they trusted me, and said I have always been a hard worker, smart, and that I never give up. I just couldn't believe it, I still can't – and it still touches my heart every time I think about it. I actually went to visit them in Gibsons recently, and they're really proud of me. It makes me feel good to have such wonderful people in my life.

That's how I got started at Support Services Unlimited. I did have to sell my car to pay the $1,500 lawyer's bill that I hadn't anticipated. I bought another car, with no money down and made monthly car payments. I guess they call that creative financing!!

My career has pretty much been computer based, in some shape or form. Before I came to Support Services I had a tendency to get bored with work very easily, and was always searching for something new and different with which to challenge myself. I never lasted at one company for more than three years. After more than eight years at SSU, I've never been bored once. Impatient, yes - things aren't moving as quickly as I'd like, but never bored. I love it, every day. I love solving problems, and figuring out a better way to do things, and trying new ideas.

Taking Over

My biggest worry when I took over SSU was that I would fail, and Bernice would have to come back from retirement to bail me out. I didn't want to let my friends and Bernice down with the money they lent me in good faith. I remember thinking it was significant that the company is as old as I am; I felt a certain amount of pride in that. I thought, oh my gosh, this company has been operating successfully for over 40 years…Denize started the company, and ran it smoothly for all those years, followed by Bernice who also did an outstanding job of things for years – I don't want to be the idiot that flushes the whole thing down the drain in six months. So that was a huge fear.

In the beginning, there were definitely lots of challenges. I had done some board work and minute taking as a volunteer secretary for my daughters' softball association, plus a little bit for the CARP annual general meeting. This didn't really prepare me for the magnitude of minute taking that was expected for the various industry types at SSU. I was very nervous about this aspect of the job. It is one thing to do minutes as a volunteer, but quite another as a paid professional.

BERNICE AND DONNA

I remember when I attended my first board meeting with Bernice for the Professional Economists. It was in a big board room on the top floor of a downtown office building; and it was very intimidating. I was literally perspiring and shaking because I was so nervous. I was glad Bernice was taking back-up notes, because everyone was talking, but I couldn't hear or understand a word they were saying – let alone take meaningful notes. I was just so nervous. To make matters worse, after the meeting, the president wanted to meet privately with Bernice and me. He proceeded to tell us that, due to budget concerns, they needed to trim back their services with SSU – and would no longer need us to take minutes. I was actually relieved, but also concerned about the loss of revenue. What a day that was!!!

Now, of course, I realize all the benefits that come from attending the board meetings. You learn so much about the association, the industry in general, and in what direction the board members want to take the association. As well, our involvement is appreciated at the meetings for much more than just recording the minutes. Normally some of the board members change each year, while we are the constant through the years and they look to us for guidance.

In the beginning I was intimidated by the prestigious class of clients we were serving. There were so many different industry types, financial planners, economists, engineers, finance, etc. These were areas that I knew absolutely nothing about and I realized quickly that there was a lot more to learn than just running a membership database. Following Bernice,

I had big shoes to fill. These associations depended on Bernice to help them run their association better, and to solve a lot of problems. It had taken her 20 years to learn everything. Were they expecting the same level of knowledge from me, right off the bat?

Money was also a huge concern in the beginning; in fact it was actually quite overwhelming. Money was coming in, but it seemed like a lot more was going out. Some of the expenses seemed huge to me. There was so much at stake – it kept me up at night worrying. I had to set aside money for GST and payroll deductions. I didn't want to damage SSU's perfect credit rating either.

We lost a few clients in the beginning, which scared me half to death, and didn't exactly boost my already low confidence level. Are they leaving because of me? Am I doing a terrible job? Are they all going to leave eventually? Keeping clients satisfied soon became the major name of the game for me.

Unfortunately, this philosophy turned out to be my undoing. I started off (and continue today) to give the clients much more in services than were actually outlined in their contract. I can never so "no", I just give them whatever they want – and rarely discuss additional costs. They all have come to expect these great services at a bargain basement price. Another problem is that when we start with a new client, the entire scope of services associated with the account is not fully recognized. And again, we end up doing more work than we get paid for. Of course, I'm notorious for never recording my time (we use the same timesheet system that Denize created 50 years ago). More free work for the client, more loss for SSU. It's been my weakness from the beginning.

I'm determined to rectify this now, and am finally becoming more business-savvy when it comes to talking contracts with clients. As we grow and take on more clients, the free work is multiplying at a rapid rate and it is impossible to keep up. I'm a volunteer at heart and money just complicates things; however running a business takes funds and this is the biggest lesson I have to learn.

Adding My Expertise

I felt confident that I could manage the databases, revamp and upgrade most of the documents with fancy text and logos. I also knew that I could save a lot of time by incorporating my sophisticated merge techniques into many of the tasks. My first order of business was to go in there and give the computer and all the documents a facelift. It was important to me to show the clients a bit of what I had to offer, the skills and abilities I could bring to the table. I was hoping to razzle-dazzle them with logos, clip-art, merging, and other computer tricks. Perhaps they wouldn't notice that I was completely inadequate in other areas.

Although I can't remember my first big success, I can certainly recall on many, many occasions feeling a great sense of pride and satisfaction that I solved a complex problem, found a better way to do something, or discovered a new product or service to benefit the association. Running SSU has really forced me to step outside my comfort zone on many levels, and I remember driving home on many occasions and thinking, wow, I can't believe I really did that today.

I don't recall which client specifically (perhaps the majority of them) but when we started putting their logos on their name badges at events they were very impressed, and we received lots of positive feedback. That was probably the first sign that my contribution was being accepted and appreciated by the clients.

The neatest thing I discovered about Support Services, was the ability to do broadcast fax. When I first met Bernice she was in the process of sending one while we spoke. Now that was cool. Considering myself fairly sophisticated when it came to computer systems, I had never seen this technology before. I was very impressed and immediately curious, and decided this was one of the first things I had to learn about. And of course, I took the broadcast fax a step further, and incorporated a logo, and personalized mail merge into each fax. One of my specialties is merging and SSU offered merge opportunities and challenges galore. I worked so many late nights at the office trying to perfect this or that, but it was always music to my ears listening to that fax sound going off. I loved it. Here I was working away plus making money on the broadcast fax at the same time.

Donna Denham

We seldom do fax blasts any more, but in the early days it was a nightly occurrence. I miss the broadcast fax; it was my best friend in those days --- keeping me company on all those late nights alone at the office. Recently we decided to revisit fax blasts because people are becoming inundated with email. Also many large company servers automatically delete emails that they suspect are spam. The fax has a better success rate of reaching the recipient, and can be passed around to others in the office. It appears to be a better marketing strategy.

A Few Problems

The most difficult part of running SSU in the beginning was deciding what to keep and what to trash. What to save on the computer and what to delete; disk space wasn't as plentiful in those days. We printed endlessly from the laser printer and our bookkeeper still uses it for printing computer cheques. That machine has been an incredible work horse and we have serviced it just twice in eight years. I kept so much paper, because I didn't know if I'd need it down the road. The paper was totally out of control at times – way too much.

Another problem was communication. When I started at SSU there was a dial-up email account, and we might get three emails a day, a big day would be 10 emails. Clients wanted communication by either email, fax, mail or a combination, and we had to accommodate all these different means of communication within each association. Email usage slowly increased over time, and we had to track changes accordingly.

Now we communicate primarily by email, but when I started it was mail-out central. It was amazing the amount of mail we processed. The two mail boxes outside the office were regularly filled to the brim from our office alone. Canada Post must have loved us. It was a big day for me when I no longer had to drive to the post office to fill the postage meter, and we could order postage by phone. MMCD (Master Municipal Construction Document Association) had one of the biggest mailing lists, far too big for the boxes outside to handle, we had to drop the mail off at the main post office, thankfully just a few blocks down Homer Street. I would also panic because I needed $1,000.00 in the bank to purchase the postage for their mailing. That kind of money wasn't easy to come by in those days. And to make it worse, it wouldn't be reimbursed until MMCD paid their SSU invoice, which might be a month later.

Bringing Back the Clients

I'm excited that some of the clients that left SSU years before I came on board, have now come back. The Canadian Club, CIPS and now QSSBC (Quantity Surveyors Society of B.C.) are back. I like that, and wonder how many others are out there. Oddly enough, Olga Barratt called recently and asked whether I knew of any fundraisers. I told her that there is an association of fundraisers and they used to work out of our office. I have a hunch that the fundraisers will be back at SSU one day soon. CSMPS (Canadian Society for Marketing Professional Services) came back and now they're gone again. Unfortunately, some associations have an operating budget that is simply too low to afford our services and they have to rely on volunteers.

So Much to Learn

At the beginning there were so many things I didn't understand. I've learned so much over the years and continue to learn new things every day. I remember when I was first with the company the printers came in about re-ordering the MMCD books. I was completely bewildered by the whole process. I even took a tour of Benwell Atkins print shop and was more confused than ever. Having to organize a wide variety of printing including brochures, newsletters, banners, and directories for our clients has helped me to learn and to keep up with new developments and pricing. Printing now offers digital, online and DVD options. SSU has been an incredible learning experience. The learning never ends!

I went to an event recently for a new client. Part of the contract asks that we set up the AV Equipment before the event. I was expecting a laptop and LCD projector - easy stuff, I thought. Boy, was I mistaken! The AV consisted of a cordless microphone, two floor mics, mixer, digital recorder, laptop, and projector all thrown together in a big box. That was interesting!!

One of my faults is being a perfectionist. I cannot rest until I've solved the problem, or made it perfect. It's never, "That's good enough". Instead, "I'll make this better, and figure this out if it takes all night." And I have done that on many occasions.

I have a tendency to grossly misjudge time. Projects often take longer than I anticipate. This happened more often when there was so much that was unfamiliar at the beginning. I didn't factor supplier time lines into the equation, not considering that all companies aren't providing same day service; they may need a week or more turn around time.

I'm still guilty of this one, but I would stay at work for hours and hours, trying to figure something out or locate new products. I would search, investigate, download and test demos, until I found the perfect product that would work for our purposes. Like broadcast email for instance. I knew it was possible, but wasn't exactly sure how. I'm going to brag a bit here; SSU was sending personalized broadcast email before most associations or companies in Vancouver even knew it existed. When I sent test emails to the clients, they were so impressed, and we started sending them out for all our clients. Then the calls came in from members, asking how we did it.

Of course I wasn't satisfied with a simple text email, I took it to the html level. I hadn't learned html in any of my computer training, but I had a rough idea of how it worked. There was a lot of self studying to make that happen. I figured it out, with the most complex task being how to insert graphics, and have them visible on the receiving end (which meant 20 different types of computers). It wasn't wasted time, because we use these emails on a daily basis for every single client. Broadcast emails are commonplace now, but eight years ago, they were really something special.

A Personal Memoir

Smokey Smith was a Victoria Cross winner who has been mentioned earlier. My grandfather died when I was a baby, but my mother told me that he was in the Second World War with Smokey at the time he won the Victoria Cross. They were good friends for years and Smokey was a pallbearer at my grandfather's funeral.

Smokey was also holder of the Order of Canada and he had been invited for several years to the Canadian Club's Order of Canada luncheon in February. He had to decline the first few invitations due to health issues, however in February 2005 he was able to come and I was very excited at the chance to meet him in person and ask him some questions about my family. Over the past few years I have enjoyed researching my family history and this was to be a wonderful opportunity to gather more information. I was extremely disappointed that I had to attend another event that day, but I thought that perhaps he might come next year. But Smokey Smith passed away on August 3, 2005, my birthday. Rest in peace Smokey.

Moving to Gastown

At last, after eight years I've felt that I've finally come into my own, and been able to fill Bernice's shoes, so to speak. The clients trust and respect my opinion and feel that their association is in good hands at Support Services. Over the years I've gained a lot of knowledge about associations, but the biggest bonus is learning so much about myself, and now having the confidence to move forward. The turning point was the move from Yaletown to Gastown. The business has quadrupled in the last eight years, and we've now tripled our office space and staff. Bernice was happy to learn that we finally hired a cleaning company. I guess that's one way to measure if you've really made it.

1107 HOMER YALETOWN OFFICE

Yaletown was growing and changing and our location at 1107 Homer was just three years short of being designated a heritage building. We loved that building and the tenants on the third floor were almost like a family. There was a travel agent, Joe Wai (the architect), an engineering company, plus Cam and David Murphy who sold medical supplies. The building had a lot of character and we were happy there. But there was the empty lot next door, and with all the construction going on in the neighbourhood, it was just a matter of time before the property would be redeveloped with condos.

I learned early in 2005 that it was being sold for demolition. We were fortunate to have a five year lease with a five option to renew, because the thought of moving and the expense involved was astronomical. We weren't looking at moving one office, but thirty. Each of our clients has a large number of members and suppliers, all of whom have to be notified of the move. All the client stationery, brochures and collateral would need to be reprinted with the new address. The address would need to be updated on each of their websites and online directories...the list goes on and on. Our rent on Homer was quite reasonable and when I started looking for a new location I looked everywhere; Yaletown, downtown, the Broadway corridor, but was looking at an increase of at least $10 per square foot no matter where it was located. This was a big undertaking and there wasn't much time. The move had to be completed during our slow period in the summer, or it wasn't going to happen. There were only a couple of months to pull this together and meanwhile we were very busy.

I didn't really want to move to Gastown because the west end of Water Street is very expensive, and if you go the other way towards Main Street it becomes a haven for panhandlers and drug addicts. One day I looked at a building being renovated just beside the Gassy Jack statue. It was a heritage building, one of the first in Gastown, with high ceilings and a view of the inlet out one side and a view of the city out the other. Unfortunately it was too early in the construction process to be ready when we needed it. Disappointed, I returned to my car and noticed a big "for lease" sign on the building that we are in now. The initial appearance was good, with heritage brick, so I called the number on the sign and the man said he would meet me in 20 minutes. When he arrived and we went inside I just fell in love with it. And this was after looking at dozens of locations in many different areas, so I knew that at last I had found what we needed. But – it was too big. The whole floor was 9,000 square feet and right away I said, "This is too big." He came back with, "We can reconfigure it."

I just had to have it. I went back to the office and told the staff. We all came down together and the place soon had everyone's approval, but still I was concerned about the size. We were in 1,000 square feet on Homer Street and the final offer from the landlord here was for 3,000 square feet. That was a bit of a stretch, but the price compared well with what we were paying on Homer. It is on the main floor, which is an advantage we didn't have at Homer. The 20 foot ceilings and floor to ceiling windows give a wonderful spacious feeling to the office, while the exposed brick and original hardwood floors let you know that the building has stood the elements for many, many years. And the best part was that we could have it organized to suit our needs. We didn't have to fit in to someone else's version of an office.

The first priority had been to find a heritage building which would remain in place as long as we needed it, because with our client list, moving is tremendously expensive.

Now it was time to go to the new building owners at Homer Street and negotiate. This was a difficult process and with little experience in this field I engaged a law firm. They eventually told me that I didn't have a leg to stand on and it would get thrown out of court if it went that far. In the end I paid the lawyer $6,000 for nothing, because I negotiated my own deal with the owners, which was substantially better than the lawyer predicted.

I studied the lease and it was clear that I had a five year option to renew and there wasn't a demolition clause to protect the interest of the owner. I was determined that this move was not going to put us out of business so that the developers could get rich building condos. They finally understood that the move was extremely complicated and expensive because of the 30 associations that used our address.

The final agreement gave us all moving expense, leasehold improvements at the new location, staff time involved to change addresses for 30 clients, plus the additional rent for the first six months in the new building. When I see Joe Wai he likes to remind me of how I played hardball with the big boys and won, and we laugh. And we run into each other often because he is now located in our building on the second floor. It is wonderful to have familiar friends in our new neighbourhood.

With that out of the way it was exciting to add a board room and kitchen to the new office. There were funds left over to furnish the board room and kitchen, and to purchase new desks and reception chairs.

However there was considerable aggravation involved with Telus, our telephone and internet service provider. Their employees were on strike and management was handling the work, however they were painfully slow. At first I wasn't concerned because we moved during our slow season and I thought we'd be up and running by September 1st. However it was almost Christmas before all of our communication services were operating efficiently.

I would stay on week-ends, waiting for them to come, because they couldn't give me a definite date. It was often, "We might be there on Saturday or Monday." So I'd wait all day Saturday and they wouldn't show. Or they would come and hook up one line but didn't seem to be able to do any more. At some point they promised to give us all cell phones and then call forward all the lines to the cell phones. Well, the invoices for the cell phones began to arrive but no phones. That provided another time consuming aggravation. Two months later the phones arrived but we no longer needed them and sent them back unopened. But still the invoices arrived and weren't finally settled until a year later.

At the same time construction was running behind schedule and wasn't finished until December. There was drywall going up and plumbing to install. Every week-end I came in and cleaned up the drywall dust because it crept in everywhere.

Growing the Business

I was feeling overwhelmed by the large amount of space we now rented and knew that we needed a lot more business to cover the added expense. With all the problems the moving generated there had been no time for marketing. We moved in August and there was enough money to keep us going until the following spring, but as the months went by I was becoming concerned because the difference in rent was $2,500 more per month. I thought, what on earth have I done? We had hired two new people and they had to share one desk for a while because our computers were also late arriving. Even the hiring process had been difficult because candidates couldn't contact us by email, phone or fax. In desperation, I used a placement agency for $7,500.

Then at the end of October a call came in from Cindy Brown. She runs a large association called Advocis from her home and had decided that she wanted to work part time, rather than full time, and she asked whether I'd like to share the contract. Then she said, "I'd like to give you part of the contract for $2,500 per month." It was "bingo"! That was exactly what we needed and it started January 1st, so that was cause for celebration! Now I could relax a bit.

Cindy had an Access database that she'd been using which we had to convert to our system. That took several months to accomplish. Then the National office decided that all regional offices must convert to the system they use, an IMIS database. This meant converting all financial info, the membership list, and event registrations, and everything now had to be processed through the national office. This created a lot of extra work and trial and error through 2006 for Cindy and I, but finally late in the year we seemed to have things worked out quite nicely.

Then in November 2006 came another call from Cindy and I was excited to speak with her. "Cindy, we've finally got it nailed down, everything is systemized and in 2007 we will just breeze through." And she said, "Well, I've got news for you. I'm retiring and don't want to work for Advocis any more. Do you want the full contract?" Wow! It turns out that we had been given the small half of a monthly contract of $6,500.00 and now we will have it all! If I had known this was likely to happen I would have paid a lot more attention to some of the details as the year went on. It was a bit of a shock, but a good surprise. Deirdre, who was on maternity leave, was returning in February and I was wondering how to cover her salary. Once again we needed to get more business and there it was.

I was happy for Cindy that she was able to retire early and pursue some of her passions. I really enjoyed working with her. She was very well respected within the Advocis group and did a fabulous job for them. Her shoes have been hard to fill, but we talk now and then and she reassures me that everything will be OK.

Since I took over this business I keep saying things like, "I should really put together a marketing plan to increase business, but the business just seems to come". I haven't done any marketing, other than the website we set up about two years ago and a small yellow pages ad. Most new business comes by word of mouth and it always seems to appear when I need it most. I remember when CAFP (one of my best clients) merged with CAIFA to become Advocis, Cindy Brown was awarded the whole contract and that was a huge loss of revenue for SSU. I was sorry to lose CAFP, but within days a call came from the BC Association of Kinesiologists, which turned out to a bigger contract than CAFP. It always seems to just happen. I don't know if it's luck or something else.

Fine Tuning

I'm satisfied to have accomplished all of the little things I set out to do, and all of my initial fears of failure are gone. The loans from Hope and Bernice have been paid, the company is still alive and growing, the credit rating is still intact, the clients are on side, and technology is one of SSU's strong points. Probably one of the most important improvements to the financial health of the company was getting the timekeeping program up and running after having it sitting on my desk for two years. Thanks to Bernice for pushing me to get it working. That was definitely a godsend in helping me invoice the clients efficiently, and to analyze the actual time we spend on their account compared to the time included in their monthly retainer. There have been big changes now that we no longer do the big mailings. We still do a certain amount of mail, particularly membership renewals, cheques, etc, as it really remains the most dependable way to communicate, and is pretty much guaranteed delivery.

I have also been pleased at the amount of credit available to us. Four years ago I had my heart set on purchasing a new and improved computer system from Dell, which cost over $50,000, and was certain that no one would give us a loan for a purchase that large. I was wrong - they were lined up at the door to give us credit, with no money down. I recently upgraded our printer/photocopier and included a colour printer. The salesman called and commented, "Do you have any idea how great your credit is? They will give you anything, your credit is fabulous!" And I thought, thank goodness! In the beginning, I was so afraid that I would damage SSU's perfect credit rating. It's time to replace the server, so we'll see if the credit is still intact.

I can't possibly explain in words how this company has changed my life. Every day is just fabulous – new people, new challenges and new experiences. What more can you ask for? I guess a little more money and a bit more free time would be nice --- that's my next challenge. I've accomplished things that eight years ago, I could never picture myself doing or even being capable of. It's been quite a journey and I've enjoyed every minute of it.

I definitely enjoy all the clients, and feel privileged to work with many kinds of personalities and styles. If by chance you happen across a difficult director, luckily you're not stuck with them forever, because the board changes every year or so, and they'll eventually be gone. I guess CARP is closest to my heart because they were with me before I bought the business, so there's some extra emotion attached to them. They are like a relative or special friend.

I'm finally starting to see the big picture about the earning potential of associations, and know that SSU is more secure with groups that can generate additional revenue over and above membership dues – so they can afford our services and benefits for their members. It helps if they have conferences, sponsorship opportunities, seminars, sell books, or provide a job posting service.

From clients there is always something to learn – we constantly take new ideas and concepts that worked for one group, and suggest that another group incorporate them. Also when one group has a bad experience we can caution others not to go down that road. The shared experience is definitely one of the benefits of using an association management company over a private contractor.

The exposure to many different professions is an eye opener; marketing, rehabilitation, kinesiology, and now Quantity Surveying (this last group was a mystery, but now I know they are part of the construction industry). It's all so amazing!! One day, I went to Victoria and back within four hours to do a venue site tour for a conference. The highlight for me was flying back at night on the heli-jet; that was fun. As we hovered over the city I felt like I was in a 3-D video game.

I love people, so it's fun to find out what business they're in and what they're doing. Often on the TV news, we'll see people we work with. Shawn Hall was a student member when we first met, and he now does public relations for Telus, often appearing on TV as their spokesman. I am constantly amazed to see members doing volunteer work for more than one association – they are a most amazing group of people, kind, generous, passionate and committed. For instance, Ron Royston (treasurer for the Canadian Club) is a partner with Grant Thornton and in his spare time works with the North Shore Search and Rescue. In that capacity he is often on TV and has actually been "knighted" for his contribution there. It is an honour for all of us at SSU to be able to assist such volunteers to shape the future of so many worthwhile organizations in this province. I take this role very seriously and want our team to provide the absolute best they can possibly offer.

I feel proud that I brought improved technology to Support Services, because that's where it needed to go in 1998. I just wish I'd met Bernice 10 years before and we could have taken Support Services globally. Seriously! Well maybe, franchised at least. I've had people ask me, "Why don't you start a company like this in Calgary or Edmonton?" If I'd met Bernice 10 years ago I believe we could have made that happen. Coincidentally, when Bernice was president of COSA, I called to get an information package. When she called back I wasn't in, and I didn't pursue any further. But if I had called again and we had met, who knows what would have happened? Just one conversation on the phone could have changed everything. It seems that we were destined to meet and I'm a better person for it.

Staffing

Teena Keizer was the employee who came with the company and provided much-needed continuity when I took over; however after 13 years with SSU she needed a change and left in mid 2006. Teena and I had a lot of fun and laughter together, and spent many long hours working side by side during my early days. She was more like a daughter to me than an employee and I appreciated her dedication to SSU. She amazed everyone with her speed on the computer. I taught her how to merge, and she became a master. We always laughed at how I first introduced her to the text box, which became an important function in formatting documents. No one can top her ability to beautifully format documents and we all miss her expertise.

Having staff is definitely interesting, and has certainly been a challenge for me. There are so many learning styles and so little time to train everyone on each aspect of the job. It's painful for the perfectionist in me to see mistakes made by new employees, but patience, encouragement and explanation seem to get us through. At the moment I have nine staff members; each with their own special capabilities which I admire and support. Our business requires incredible teamwork and foolproof systems. Everyone in the office is involved in each project and our systems must make everything meld perfectly. I've started to devote more time and interest to staff training and morale. We have weekly team meetings over lunch so everyone can learn more about each other, the clients, new processes, what's happening the following week, and talk about concerns or find solutions.

Deirdre Taylor came back from maternity leave in February 2007 and is our project/office manager. She is a positive person with excellent communication skills. She is the perfect ambassador for SSU and is well liked by both staff and clients.

Doreen Muir does accounting and she is the best in the business. She has never missed a deadline and approaches her work with both dedication and a happy disposition. We bought her flowers recently after she stayed all night until 5:30 am to finish statements for clients. You don't find dedication like that every day!

I'm very excited to have Naomi Liu on board, handling graphics and website development. Her skills and abilities have improved the service we can offer clients by 100%. She is also a professional photographer, which is a bonus. Photography is her passion and she is pleased to have the opportunity to use this talent at SSU.

Suzanne Wallace is receptionist and handles all the event registrations. She has come a very long way in confidence and abilities, and I'm so proud of her. She takes great pride in her work, and has excellent time management and organizational skills. She is a valued part of the team.

Sarah Le is responsible for membership. She is a brilliant woman with a great attention to detail, and we look forward to big improvements in the membership department very soon.

Ashlee King is our communications coordinator, handling minutes, thank you letters and newsletters. Writing is her passion and it definitely shows, as her work is beautifully composed.

Devon Miller is my youngest daughter, and is primarily responsible for production, as well as many miscellaneous tasks; banking, compiling feedback forms, event registration and helping me with lots of crazy projects.

Lee-Ann Denham is another of my daughters and she is a floater, filling in where needed. She has a natural math and logic aptitude which has been especially useful for creating many of the new systems we developed in the office.

We recently hired Christina Meierl as finance administrator. She will assist Doreen with bookkeeping duties, as well as wrap-up all the events, accounts receivable, invoicing and payment processing. Christina was working across the hall at a clothing manufacturer. When the company moved their operation to China she became available.

FROM L-R: NAOMI LIU, DAN TAYLOR, DEIRDRE TAYLOR, ASHLEE KING, DEVON MILLER, ERICK STEELE, DONNA DENHAM, SUZANNE WALLACE, SARAH LE, LEE-ANN DENHAM

With all the new clients and staff we really need Deirdre to manage the day to day operations. There is a steep learning curve for new people and it takes some time before they understand the complexity of what SSU is all about. Deirdre runs the team meetings, coaches new hires to ensure that they are trained properly, and she will deal with other challenges as they arise. SSU has grown beyond my ability to handle all the details and Deirdre is doing a fabulous job of filling that void.

With the help of my daughter Lee-Ann, we've set up many effective systems that make the work much easier to do as well as understand. The procedure manual that Bernice developed has now been converted to Microsoft One-Note, which is a computerized index binder. We recently developed job descriptions, so everyone knows their basic job responsibilities, and that of the others in the office. The jobs are set up in a department style, which is designed to allow everyone to play a part in client activities, and also to limit the chance of competition amongst the staff. The teamwork aspect is critically important with this type of system. I love that we now have a wide selection of perspectives and talent, with many skills and abilities that are superior to mine. We take pride in encouraging staff to utilize their strengths and abilities. With the diversity of work and crazy projects at SSU, everyone has an opportunity to shine at something different and try new things, often uncovering hidden abilities.

Our office is easy going, relaxed and fun. My space is always open to everyone and they can talk to me about anything. Nothing is off limits; they are welcome to know anything about the business, within privacy law regulations. Everyone who visits or calls our office is acknowledged with kindness and treated with respect, including couriers, janitors and presidents…everyone, no exceptions. The same principles that Denize used 50 years ago are still practiced today. We pride ourselves on offering friendly, affordable and efficient service, and we stand by it.

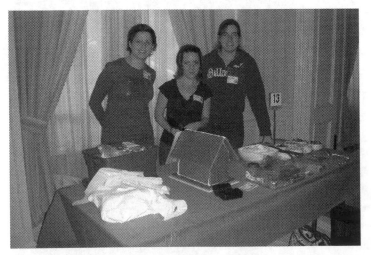

FROM L-R: SARAH LE, ASHLEE KING, LEE-ANN DENHAM.
GINGERBREAD HOUSE DECORATING CONTEST AT THE SUTTON HOTEL

MARGOT THE BULLDOG

In 2007 Denize might be surprised to learn that some of us can connect to the office server from our home computers. We regularly have dogs stay in our office; Ashlee has a cute little pug named Jack resting on her lap for at least three hours a day, and she takes him for a walk at lunch time. There is no rule about eating or drinking at our desks and kids are welcome to spend the day at the office when they don't have school. We wear bare feet and sandals to work, jeans on Fridays and regularly rock to 80's music to jump start the morale. We talked today about doing Margarita Mondays (virgin, of course). Some of our staff have tattoos and unusual piercings (hidden, naturally) and I notice that some of our female clients also sport tattoos. We now offer a benefit package and are always flexible with family and personal obligations.

Equipment and Systems

I had spent a great deal of time with David Finley, to set up our database to do more than just track members' names and addresses. David had been working with our databases since the early 90's so he was familiar with our clients. We added ability to track attendance at events, to print name tags, to email receipts for member dues and events etc. It is quite sophisticated; cuts down on time necessary and streamlines everything. Each client has their own database; however once you know one client you know them all because the format is the same.

DAVID FINLEY AT 1107 HOMER, 1998

We use Simply Accounting for almost everyone, with just one client on Quickbooks. We have software for pretty much everything, but the database is the key.

Technology has taken off in the past five years and it's amazing what is available. The copier we had on Homer Street was reaching the end of the contract at the time we were preparing to move. It had the ability to send faxes, print from all the computers in the office, collate and staple as well as make a single photocopy. The replacement does all that plus makes pdfs and scans typed copy into a word document which can be edited. Our photocopy needs have been decreasing, while we do more printing from our computers with no system to charge this printing to the client. The new machine is a network printer as well, so each page can be charged to the client and documented electronically. Every fax is counted, every scan is counted, as well as each photocopy. It also makes little saddle stitched books, which are perfect for an AGM. We put a little voting card in, along with reports and financial statements and these booklets are a big hit.

Along with the copier, and for the same price we had been paying, we added a colour laser printer. We don't use it a lot but it works well for badges and this excited me because I wanted the name badges to have a punch of colour. Also, for some clients who don't have letterhead, we can produce small runs of coloured letterhead at very low cost.

New Products and Services

The next challenge for us moving forward is on-line services, which I'm starting to research. My criteria are:

- It has to be an improvement over our current systems
- It has to make money for SSU

It's not good business to be working more efficiently and making less money. Technology has saved our clients so much when you compare postage versus email. Mail is time consuming to prepare.

> Email announcements for an average client cost $50, compared to $500 for a mailing

Technology has given our clients more money to spend on other initiatives. I try to incorporate technology advantages in every way possible, such as using on-line surveys rather than printing on paper, with results compiled automatically. On-line registration and on-line credit card processing allows for pre-payment for events, rather than at the door. All of this is fast and efficient.

This is good news for the client but bad news for us, as we provide much more in the way of service for the same amount of money. I'm all for automation, but it is definitely not putting SSU on the Fortune 500 list.

Our next challenge is the web and there's some great material there, but not everything is useful. We use on line databases for a few of our clients, but find them totally inferior to our in-house database. Ours has a huge number of options – you can group people, email them a personalized invoice or receipt in PDF, process credit cards, print envelopes, attendance lists, run meaningful reports. Most web material is not very flexible or won't fit perfectly for our needs, and the good stuff is very expensive. I'm starting to notice that products are improving slowly and are coming down in price a bit. Hopefully, we'll get there soon.

The thing about Support Services is that it's almost impossible to buy something in a box, off the shelf. If you have just one company, it's easy. In our case, it has to work for 30 different clients. It's always a challenge finding software that is going to work for our purposes. Every product that we purchase has to be tested and re-tested to ensure it will work equally for all clients. It has to be flexible. When I finally purchased our time-keeping program, I tried out almost a hundred programs before deciding. Recently, I was feeling a bit down, thinking that I haven't done enough, and things aren't moving quickly enough. I started to write a list of all the improvements that I've introduced over the years, with the majority of them technology based. It gave me a little boost, as the list was fairly long.

My Business Philosophy

I consider myself a workhorse, not a showhorse. I am basically shy, and most comfortable being in the background. I don't require recognition for accomplishments, as I have my own ways of measuring success with clients and SSU to ensure the results expected are achieved. My team enjoys being appreciated, so I like them to receive the accolades. Self-motivated and curious by nature, I enjoy learning and challenges and always attempt to improve and make a difference where I can. I sincerely care about people and am always fair, honest and genuine with everyone.

My daughters tell me I'm a risk taker. I agree that I've taken many financial risks at SSU, but they have been somewhat calculated, and luckily they all worked out.

Lately, it's really started to hit home that I lack business savvy when it comes to making money. I've taken personal inventory, and realize that I've never put much emphasis on money. This makes me wonder why I'm running a business, because it's obviously not for the money, or for the prestige. I've come to the conclusion that it's the work, people, and the honour of being a part of SSU that keeps me going. My desire is for the entire SSU team to share the same passion. I'm also on a mission to continue moving SSU to where I envision it. I think it may be close, just about everything is in place. It's now up to talented and committed staff to help us get there. Perhaps the financial pay off will follow. You never know.

I consider my staff as family, and really enjoy having my daughters at the office. I've spent so much time there over the years, which meant missing a lot of important time with them in the past. I enjoy having them at the office with me and love watching them develop. I drive in to work with Devon every morning, and we chat about life, and her friends, her latest boyfriend, and this is so special to me. As long as my daughters want to stay at SSU I'm thrilled to have them. I feel privileged to uphold the long tradition of family involvement within our organization.

I don't have an exit strategy, but that will come in time. With nothing put away for retirement, and every penny I've earned re-invested in SSU, I am preparing myself mentally for the possibility of working until I'm 80, but would much prefer to retire in my early 60's. I know that I must work smarter for the next 15 years, if I expect to retire with any security. I am concerned about who would take it over; how much it would sell for. This is a long time span, especially in terms of technology impacting our type of business. Who knows, maybe in 15 years, SSU will be all virtual, no office, just a web presence with programmers in India running the operation. Of course, I would love one of my daughters to carry on, but it is unlikely they would. Perhaps Deirdre would be in a position to take it over; in 15 years her boys will be all grown up. I'd like that very much.

SSU is such a unique company, the work is so interesting and challenging that staff seem to stay on for longer than with many other companies. I would really love to see the right person take over SSU when I'm gone, and keep the legacy going for another 50 years. It's not easy for someone to walk into this business off the street and expect to understand all the many details that are involved. For instance Bernice had worked in the business before she became a partner; I had background in association management when I bought the business, and with Bernice staying on part-time, I had a back up. I'll cross that bridge when I get a bit closer, and rely on fate to send the right person my way.

Hope and Bernice are the first I need to thank, I'm grateful to them for believing I could actually do it, and trusting me with an awful lot of money. Without them, I wouldn't have the business to begin with. Bernice is one of the greatest people I've ever met, I admire her immensely. I learned everything from her, and consider her my friend, confidant and mentor. There are a lot of people who have sent business my way, and have given me excellent tips and advice on how to run the business. Even Bernice's contacts from previous years continue to support me and SSU. So many people I've met are genuinely happy to see the business doing well and are very supportive. I always try to give back, and support other small businesses, especially those that have helped me along the way. We use a lot of services and I have the opportunity to send work to people who will do a good job.

The move to Gastown really put me on my own. Bernice left just before we moved and Teena soon after and now the company seems more like my own because I have created the architecture and hired all the staff. In February 2006, the construction was complete, the drywall dust finally settled, the phones were working and business was normal again. It was time for a celebration. We combined Bernice's retirement party with an open house, and the Gastown office was a perfect party place. This was the first party I had organized since taking over the business. I knew SSU had a reputation for putting on great parties, so I was excited to finally do one of my own. We had the best time ever. There were beautiful flower arrangements all over the office, catered food, open bar, a characterist sketched portraits for all the guests, door prizes, gifts, party favours, cake, doormen, coatracks, music, videos, guest book…the works. About 200 guests arrived, with a mixture of old and new SSU staff and clients, family, friends, neighbours. We had a professional photographer taking pictures all night, but the camera malfunctioned and none of the pictures turned out. The weather wasn't great that night, and unfortunately Denize was unable to make the trip. It would have been fun to have the three of us together again. I'm ready to party again at the 50 year anniversary

Support Services has managed to maintain a reputation of being a highly respected small business in Vancouver. It is staggering to consider the magnitude of professionals and companies from every sector possible that have come in contact with SSU in some way or other over the last 50 years. I'm not sure that many small service businesses can make that claim. When we moved to Gastown, we sent over 60,000 change of address notifications comprised of all the association's members and suppliers. The company has a character and a presence all of its own, almost like a separate entity with amazing momentum. It's important to me to maintain the original reputation, values, client service and satisfaction at the highest level. I hope it will keep going long after I'm done with it. Denize had her term, Bernice had her term and I hope to have at least 20 years to make my contribution.

It's a unique business with a great reputation. So many people know the company and respect it. I overheard someone at a dinner meeting recently talking about our company. A lot of people say, "I know Support Services, or I used to know someone who was a client." The clients are certainly loyal, Don Thomas still sends us his Christmas letter, but it's now distributed by email. We've recently been doing some ongoing projects for Poul Hansen who told me that he has been doing business with Tri-C since Denize was the owner, and he's always received excellent service throughout the years. The fact that he continues to support our company makes me feel good.

Chapter Eight
THE SUMMING UP

*A*nd now we are in 2007 and the 50th anniversary. What a journey it's been, with many fourteen hour days; yet each of the owners has found great satisfaction in their work. And each of them exhibited the following qualities:

1.   Courage

Denize had the courage to walk along the street and go into offices to promote the business when she started it in 1957. Then 21 years later she made a huge upgrade from 1,000 square feet to 5,000 and enlarged the concept from a secretarial service to a packaged office.

Bernice had the courage to take the company in a new direction in 1991, just as the trend to home-based offices began. She downsized space to 1,000 square feet and focused on building the association management sector of the business.

Donna had the courage to expand the space and in 2005 moved to 3,000 square feet and within a year had triple the business and staff that she had begun with in 1998.

2.   Independence

Each of these women had to earn a living, as none of them had either spousal or parental support. They all valued their independence and enjoyed making decisions and providing leadership to others.

3.   Creativity

These women showed practical creativity. They could envision their business in a new setting, and then begin to work to make it happen. Sometimes this happened in spite of the caution advocated by others, i.e., when Denize applied to rent the entire ground floor at 1250 Homer, the Atkins brothers (her landlords) tried to dissuade her.

4.   Integrity

When these women gave their word you could count on it, even if they had to work through the night to accomplish a task.

5.   Open to Learning

Each of these women knew that they didn't know it all and continued to learn through their whole lives. Donna loves to sit down and "figure it out for herself". Bernice has taken courses her whole life and now teaches at Eldercollege. Denize learned from her clients and by asking questions of colleagues.

6.   Enjoys Living on the Edge

When there's a challenge in front of them, these women go for it, and problems become opportunities. The necessity to move to new premises always encouraged them to come up with something new and better.

7.   Varied Work Experience

Each of these women had a good business background and had learned from the varied experience that was available to them. They weren't the type to "just do their job" when working for someone else, but gave their very best and enjoyed being productive.

WHAT PROVIDED THE MOST SATISFACTION?

Denize
- enjoyed helping young people develop, i.e. Valerie Jenkinson
- enjoyed being part of larger national and international companies
- enjoyed the wide range of contacts that she developed
- enjoyed her home and her horses in Pemberton on weekends

Bernice
- enjoyed the challenges of living on the edge
- enjoyed learning through association with highly capable people
- enjoyed hiring young people out of school and watching them develop
- enjoyed being able to buy a home and travel

Donna
- enjoyed bringing major technology upgrades
- enjoyed paying off acquisition loans and maintaining the company's credit record
- enjoyed growing the business since she took it over
- enjoyed having her daughters work with her in the business

All of this was accomplished by women who began without financial resources. Denize began by bartering some of her services for office space. Both Bernice and Donna financed their purchase with borrowed funds. From this we can see that integrity plays a huge role. These women had to be "as good as their word", because that was all that they had. Yet in their hearts they knew that they could and would make it.

EPILOGUE

Donna has suggested that some people who read this book may wish to know what Denize and Bernice are doing these days.

Denize

In October of 1984 Denize moved from her west end apartment to Pemberton on a permanent basis, rather than being a week-ender in that beautiful valley. When she first saw the area in 1967 she said to her friends and family, "I never want to leave this valley." That was when she began to plan her retirement.

The first year was spent at home there, and she was soon shoveling snow, splitting fire-wood, shoveling more snow and cross-country skiing. By the next October she was re-energized and decided to become an active member of the community.

Her volunteer activities included church work in Pemberton, Whistler and Mount Currie, under one Priest, her good and dear friend Fr. Wilfred Scott. He was replaced by Fr. Bob Haggarty, with whom she worked on plans for a new church and rectory in Whistler. In the mid-nineties these buildings were completed and dedicated.

Denize improved her culinary talents, which had been long dormant, by joining the Ladies Auxiliary to the Royal Canadian Legion, as this group did a lot of catering within the community, including dinners and Christmas parties. In her volunteer work with the Pemberton & District Museum and

Archives Society, she used the skills honed during her days at Tri-C. In later years she has worked with the Pemberton Valley Seniors Society.

Over the past 20 years Denize has continued to travel, spending time in Egypt, Israel, Spain, France, Italy, England and Dubai; either visiting family and friends, tracing family roots or just being a tourist. Life continues to be very fulfilling and rewarding and she is most thankful for good health, good friends and close family connections.

Bernice

First on Bernice's agenda when she sold the business in 1998 was a long wished-for trip to Europe, where she began in Athens, then went to Crete, Rome, Monte Carlo, Paris, Amsterdam and London in March and April of 1999.

Then she began to write her life story, inspired by the memoirs of Francis Wright. It took a year to complete but was such a satisfying journey that she wanted to show others the way. Soon a workshop had been created and several of her friends formed a pilot project. In time she joined the Association of Personal Historians and learned how to interview people in order to publish their life story. This has become a wonderful passion and now seems more important than all the traveling she had planned to do.

Her volunteer activities have been with Canadian Women's Voters Congress, which runs an annual campaign school for women in conjunction with UBC. She served two terms as their President and was honoured by an invitation to be keynote speaker at Yale University for their Women's Campaign School in 2005. She also volunteers with Palliative Care at Lions Gate Hospital in North Vancouver.

She enjoys Scottish Country Dancing and Scrabble and plans to visit Russia next year.

BERNICE AND BART BROOKS

APPENDIX I – Locations

Denize Callaway began Tri-C Secretarial Services at the corner of Georgia and Cardero in 1957. She moved next door two years later and rented space on the ground floor, then later took over several offices on the second floor, which formed the beginning of her "packaged offices".

In 1968 Denize moved the company to the 1200 block of Burrard Street as the premises she was using were to be demolished. In this location she had offices on two floors.

In 1978 Denize organized a major expansion with the move to 1250 Homer Street and a five-fold increase in space. Here there were 16 offices on the periphery of the main floor and space in the main part of the office for Denize and three employees in the front half of the floor and desk space in the rear for those who didn't need a full office. Shortly after the move the company became Tri-C Secretarial Services Inc.

It wasn't until 1991 that Bernice Davidson engineered the next move to 1107 Homer and again the overall structure was changed. Space was reduced from 5,000 square feet to 1,100 square feet and the packaged office became an association management company. At this time the operating name changed to Support Services Unlimited, however the legal name remains the same.

Demolition of most of the old buildings in Yaletown eventually reached 1107 Homer and in 2005 Donna Denham took the company to Gastown with an address at 211 Columbia Street.

APPENDIX II – Equipment & Systems

The best way to illustrate the changes over 50 years is to look at the work involved in organizing a meeting. As an example we will arrange a monthly breakfast meeting for an association client where the expected attendance is 40 people.

The 1960 office is staffed by two people.

Equipment:
- two manual typewriters
- Gestetner for printing
- one rotary dial phone

To begin, we pick up a new cardboard file folder and write the name of the client and the date of the event on the tab.

The first task is to find a speaker. In most cases a director will give us the names of two or three possible speakers. We will pick up our rotary dial telephone and in most cases call a secretary to inquire whether Mr. Big is available on the date of our scheduled meeting. A note then goes into the file about when we expect an answer. When an affirmative answer is received we ask the secretary to mail us a bio and the title of the speech.

Now we can call the hotel and confirm our date for this event, giving the expected attendance and the menu we wish to serve. The hotel will mail us two copies of a contract for the event and we sign one and mail it back to the hotel, while our copy goes into the file.

Meanwhile we will prepare envelopes for the mailing, which will be sent to all the members. First we pull out the master mailing list for the association and check to see if anyone has moved over the past month. If they have we use white-out on that person's address and type in the new address. We then type an envelope for each member, copying from that list.

When the speaker's bio arrives we compose a notice for the event, asking people to telephone us to reserve a seat, or to mail us a cheque to pay in advance. This is typed on to a Gestetner master sheet and the number of copies we need is run off (about 100).

The mailing notice is processed quickly as follows:

- folded in batches (never one by one), using a folding bone
- line up envelopes to insert notice
- dampen glue with sponge, seal
- reverse envelopes, line up 10 at a time to affix stamps
- bundle in batches with rubber bands and take to mailbox

Next we set up a sheet in the file to take reservations, adding names as phone calls come in and as cheques are received in the mail. We also note that some reservations were paid in advance, and then their cheques go into the vault for safe keeping until we do a bank deposit after the event.

Two days before the breakfast we phone the hotel to guarantee the number of people that will be attending. We go to the bank and pick up cash for a float, then check that we have enough sticky name badges for the people attending. Next day we type up an attendance list, putting people's names in alphabetical order.

The person going to the breakfast puts everything needed in the briefcase before leaving the office the night before, and then is at the hotel bright and early at 7:00 am the next morning, in a dress and high heels and a big smile. People check in and receive a receipt (hand written of course).

When we come into the office the first thing to do is count the money, deduct the float, and reconcile the cash and cheques. Then it's a trip to the bank to deposit all the receipts for that event, after hand writing the deposit. If there were no shows we type up invoices and send them out in the mail that night. Our reconciliation will show any outstanding receivables.

All of this would take approximately 16 hours.

Now let's fast forward to 1982

The office is now staffed by five people.

Equipment:
- five telephones with push buttons
- four electric typewriters with correcting tape

- a postage meter
- one word processor
- an early fax machine
- two photocopiers
- one telex machine

Some things remain the same. We still pull out a cardboard file folder to accumulate items for the event. We still phone the speaker and the hotel.

However, now we receive the speaker bio and hotel contract by fax – they are there within the hour. Amazing!

We no longer type envelopes. The master membership list is set up so that it can be put in the copier and names and addresses are copied on to labels. How much easier that is than typing each one individually. The meeting notice is still typed but copying takes no time at all. In fact the copies will be printed while we apply the labels to the envelopes. Then we still do the old fold and stuff routine. Sealing and stamping is now processed by the postage meter.

Reservations are handled the same way, however the copier makes it much easier to produce receipts. They are typed up, three to a sheet, photocopied and cut with the heavy duty paper cutter - much easier than hand writing each one.

We are still going to the bank for a float and phoning the hotel with our guarantee. And we still dress up to go to the breakfast in the morning; however one person can now handle a larger crowd as she doesn't have to hand write receipts.

Back at the office we do the reconciliation the same way; however deposits go to the bank by courier, as this costs the client less than sending a staff person to wait in line to make a deposit. Most of the time savings can be attributed to the photocopier. It now takes 12 hours to handle the same type of event.

Now we are in 2007 and things have really changed.

The office is now staffed by twelve people.

Equipment
- twelve computers (typewriters and telex are long gone)

- photocopier/printer/fax
- postage meter (much less usage than previously)
- twelve telephones plus speaker phone in board room
- *The internet is here!*
- The event folder is now in the computer with all details.
- We still phone a speaker and the hotel.
- We receive an electronic picture of the speaker which is incorporated into the meeting notice.
- Meeting notice is sent electronically (no more envelopes or folding and stuffing).
- Something new: after the attendance list is input, name badges can be generated – these include the client logo
- Receipts are sent by email
- Also all events require payment in advance – no more going to the bank for a float.
- Most payment is by charge card, deposited directly to the client's bank account via the internet. Any cheques received are sent to the bank by courier.

We are now down to 8 hours, primarily because of the internet.

Not only do clients pay for much less labour time, they have the benefit of much more sophisticated service:

- pictures and logos on meeting notice
- logo on name tags, receipts and invoices
- no printing or postage cost
- no-shows are paid in advance, so no lost revenue

Event notice sent to 100 people, 40 is expected attendance for breakfast

Phone calls	.75 hr	Pack items for hotel	.50 hr
Input, distribute notice	1.50 hr	Travel to & from	.50 hr
Take reserves	.50 hr	Registration	1.50 hr
Input attendance list	.50 hr	Reconcile	1.00 hr
Generate receipts	.25 hr	Bank deposit	.50 hr
Generate name tags	.50 hr		

APPENDIX III - Marketing

Mickey had great sales experience and Denize couldn't have had a better teacher to tell her how to go out and find work. She had a lot of experience in various industries, and good organizational ability, along with being a good secretary with shorthand. She just started out walking up and down Georgia Street, knocking on doors, walking into offices, having a tough struggle to get by the secretaries in some places. Once she was able to convince them that she was there so that they wouldn't have to work so hard and if they didn't want to do overtime they could send work down the street to her, things became a bit easier.

Over the years Denize talked about her business to almost everyone she met, whether in a business or social context. She had created a unique concept and people found it interesting and useful. By 1960 she still made the odd sales call and continued her PR, but most of the work, once she started, was from people saying "Go to Tri-C" and that's how it went. Architectural and accounting and sales people with offices in eastern Canada became the company's staple clientele; people who paid the rent and the phones, and then as Denize expanded, there was more money coming in.

Word of mouth served Tri-C well, both for finding employees and for finding new customers. Even the Serra Club, which was the first association, was made up of people who needed other services. Theses for university students, whose parents were members, were typed and soon the word spread at the university that Tri-C was available to do that kind of work.

Another thing that Denize picked up along the way was effective placement in the Yellow Pages. She found that by listing the company under *A D Callaway, Tri-C Secretarial Services*, brought in lots of work. Had it been listed the other way around it would have been near the bottom of the list. Under Public Stenographers Denize's name was usually the first one on the page. Many people begin at the top of the list when looking for a service such as Tri-C offered and don't look any further.

Denize never found it necessary to pay for advertising but she spent a lot of time talking about the company to everybody she met. It is amazing how quickly she met a lot of people, and through Mickey and Pacific Western Airlines there was exposure to people on the go. In the 1950's airline travel was not nearly as common as it is today. Most people using airlines in those days were the 'movers and shakers' of the business community. One of the pilots had a riding stable in the Cariboo and she had stayed there. When they needed brochures they came to her. It seemed as if wherever she went there was an opportunity for her to promote the business and pick up some work.

Personally Denize has a lot of faith in God and she believed that she could be successful. With hard work success did come her way and she believes that it was meant to be. She doesn't give destiny total credit, but does give credit to the type of people she met and learned from. Other factors came into play, such as the quality of work which was consistent, and the fact that the customer was always treated with a great deal of respect. Each person was acknowledged when they came into the office and that created good public relations and brought in new customers. If someone was busy typing 100 words a minute they would look up and acknowledge that someone was there and the customer knew that they had been accepted. It was the same with telephones; they were always answered, even if you were put on hold. The office was busier than most places, yet Denize found that staff members were more comfortable if they could acknowledge people. Everyone was made to feel welcome when they came into the office.

BERNICE, MARLIES (LAST 2 ON LEFT) AND CHRISTINE MCGUIRE
(MARLIES' DAUGHTER LAST ON RIGHT)
WHITE WATER RAFTING AT BEND, OREGON DURING SME REGIONAL CONFERENCE

Over the years SME provided many opportunities to hear the best motivational speakers in North America and what a privilege that was! Both Denize and Bernice learned marketing tips from some of the best in the business world. Bernice attended conferences in San Francisco and Dallas, and then hosted SME's International Conference in Vancouver in 1986. There were also regional conferences which combined learning with fun and good fellowship. What a privilege to be paid to listen to information on how to market the business.

ANNETTE IN ELF SUIT

For two years Bernice promoted "Letters from Santa" at Christmas time. It seemed like a good concept as the office slowed down in December and this appeared to be a good fill-in. In the second year it was promoted at a conference aimed at parents of small children. Annette was dressed as an elf in a red velvet rental suit and she loved doing this promotion, however the results were disappointing. Then someone found out that employees at the post office answered letters on behalf of Santa – and they did it for free! We couldn't compete with that and the lesson to be learned here is to do more research before offering a new service.

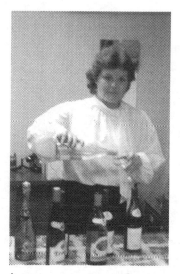

IRENE AS BARTENDER AT CHRISTMAS PARTY

Marketing includes keeping current clients happy and through the years there was at least one party per year where clients were invited to come in for a glass of wine and some finger food. This happened just before Christmas, again a good time of year to plan a party as there is a definite slow-down of business in the latter half of the month. Also, it gave the employees, and even some clients like Ron Gamble, the opportunity to show off their culinary talents. And none of those dinky little plastic glasses – it is important to rent proper wine glasses for such an event.

you're invited to our
Christmas Party!
Tuesday December 16, 1980
5:30 P.M.-8:00 P.M.
Tri-C Secretarial Services

Another promotional idea was to have an "Association Night" where each of the client associations had an opportunity to "show their wares" to our entire client base. There was also space for other clients and service providers to set up a booth showing the services they could offer to associations. Tri-C's tenants were particularly interested to see what various groups offered, while the association members enjoyed meeting people who did printing or created brochures. And our old friend, Tor Bengtson of SME, came along to take some wonderful pictures.

After the move to 1107 Homer Street it was time for an aggressive marketing campaign. The first step was a letter to the directors of each of the associations that the company managed. Although there were only about seven or eight associations at that time, this translated to almost 150 contacts, and most of those people were considered "well connected". This announced our move and invited them to think about our capabilities for any other group they worked with.

Next Bernice began working with Michael Gerber's staff, learning how to grow the business. And it was here that the new name came into being and was announced for July 1, 1992. The company was now "Support Services Unlimited" to reflect the new range of services which were more management, rather than administrative. A news release to reflect the change was a good way to get the new name in the various newspapers.

Donna relates that whenever a new client comes in they almost always say, "I never knew such a business existed, that there is a company that handles all of these tasks." This makes her think that if she did some serious marketing it could really take off. Now that she's past the stage of running by the seat of her pants, that time may come, and when it does – watch out world!